Fast, Cheap, and Good

Sustainability, One Choice at a Time

Jennifer Patterson Lorenzetti

DEDICATION

For my parents, Michael and Janice Patterson, who taught me
everything I know about living independently. And for my husband
Daniel ("Mr. FC&G"), who lives the life with me.

Contents

1 Introduction.. 1

2 Philosophy 5

3 Gardening 27

4 Recipes.. 37

5 Food Preservation... 101

6 Textiles 119

7 Household Helps 135

8 Preparing for the Worst...................................... 163

Appendix: Index.. 171

1 Introduction

I have been an independent writer for many years, and more than once I have encountered a client or editor who seemed to want the world in no time flat, all for a rock bottom price.

"Fine," I mutter as I get off the phone. "Pick any two: fast, cheap, or good."

It is a fact of small business life that the entrepreneur must enforce these hard choices with the client; a successful business owner typically must keep a full queue of work just to survive, and those clients who would like a rush job or some extra attention given their project must be willing to pay for the late nights and the need to turn down other potential projects. And until someone is able to fix that pesky "24 hours in a day" thing, entrepreneurs will need to make smart decisions about how they sell their time and service.

However, I think things are a bit different when the topic switches to sustainable living. I'm not the first to break the news that the U.S. economy has weathered an economic upheaval that will have aftershocks for years to come, and more of us are recognizing the need to make changes in how we run our homes that increase our independence, decrease our need to rely on outside sources (whether that be business or government), and respect local providers as well as our planet. We want to do these things for our health, for our pocketbook, and because they just feel good.

But, see the time problem above. None of us has unlimited time, and a program of sustainability in which we have to quit our jobs, master complicated techniques, or give up the pleasures of life is, well, unsustainable.

Hence, "Fast, Cheap, and Good," a blog that I have run successfully since 2009. This book is a compilation of some of the most popular posts in the first three years of the blog, edited and updated.

(A note about prices: When I have completed price calculations, I have typically left the prices as they were at the time the original blog post was written. Overall, prices have gone up on most goods, which means that the savings that come from a sustainable substitute will likely be more than the original calculations suggest. Think of the original prices as an "at least" in terms of savings.)

In the pages that follow, I will be detailing the steps you can take to save money and time in your housekeeping endeavors -- shopping, cooking, food provision, cleaning, sewing, and the like -- all with the following goals in mind. Tips must be:

Fast: If a project takes up an entire day, you are unlikely to undertake it more than occasionally. Therefore, most of these tips will be quick to institute and complete, with little start-up effort involved. For projects that actually do eat up some time, most of that time will allow for multitasking. (Think bread baking; it takes a couple of hours, but you don't actually have to stand there and watch the stuff rise.)

Cheap: At no time will I be asking you to run to the store for caviar and foie gras to complete a recipe or project. These projects will help your budget, either immediately or in the long run. The results of these projects should either cost less than the store-bought versions, or ultimately result in savings for you, your family, or your community and environment.

Good: Good is in the eye of the beholder, of course, but these projects are intended to improve your life, not diminish it. No cardboard cuisine or sloppy rags masquerading as frugal clothing. Each project should be tasty, attractive, or of better quality than a mass-produced version, and each should increase enjoyment and/or health for you and your family and be responsible for your community and environment.

I'll try to make an honest assessment of each project along these lines and see how close I can get to helping you make your life "fast, cheap, and good."

Let's get started!

A Word About History

When I'm not writing, gardening, or keeping house, I put on my other hat: history professor. As an adjunct prof. at a local college, I'm fascinated by the way people lived in prior decades and centuries.

Before the ubiquity of the internet, television, or even radio, intrepid pioneers settled this country with very little in the way of reference material to draw on. Frequently, what we would think of as a "cookbook" was really a household management manual, filled with recipes, cleaning instructions, medical knowledge (since the line between first aid and actual medical care was pretty blurry), and hints on the economy of running a home. The inclusion of these types of tips and articles was so successful that many decades of later, true cookbooks still included a section at the back called "household helps" or something similar.

I invite you to think of this book as an homage to these earlier household guides. In it, you will find tips, philosophies, recipes, and best practices. Although it is divided into sections by topic, I invite you to read it more randomly, picking a project here or a recipe there to try. As with the original pioneers who settled this country, your journey belongs to you and you alone.

2 Philosophy

Most people embrace a sustainable lifestyle because it fits with their philosophy, but you don't have to be a deep thinker to find a lot of good ideas in the sustainable living community.

- Do you care about saving money for your retirement, for your children, or for your next vacation? That's part of sustainability.

- Do you value being able to do things for yourself? That's part of sustainability.

- Do you wish you had some of the skills your grandparents or great-grandparents had? That's part of sustainability.

- Do you want to preserve natural resources for generations to come? That's part of sustainability.

- Do you cringe at the idea of waste? That's part of sustainability.

In this section, I explore some of the philosophical reasons to embrace a sustainable lifestyle. I hope these give you some inspiration; I hope you find some ideas of your own, as well.

What is Sustainability?

The vocabulary used in talking about sustainable living is fluid. Academics will use terms one way, those with a political perspective another, and those just chatting over the back fence still another. While there will be some commonalities among them all, I wanted to share the personal definition that I use so you know what I mean when I write.

Sustainability: If something is "sustainable," that literally means that it can be sustained, or continued. I use this term to indicate a practice that can be continued indefinitely with the resources on hand or with those that can be reasonably expected. For example, if I plan to buy a house, I need to either pay for it with cash on hand (without depleting emergency and retirement funds), or I need to only take a mortgage I can anticipate being able to service from earnings or savings for quite some time, even if I or Mr. FC&G lose clients, become unemployed, or have to tap our funds for another reason. This will obviously result in our buying a house that is far less expensive than what the mortgage broker would tell us we qualify for (trust me on this!), but the expense is *sustainable*.

There are four major categories of resources I consider on my blog and in this book, and they explicitly or implicitly are reflected in the FC&G analysis:

Health: Your health is paramount. It is a resource that, once lost, is difficult to get back. I could tell you to save money by eating off a famous golden arches dollar menu, but that would not sustain your health. I often will tell you to eat organic, even if it means greater expense or greater time out in the garden (which is exercise to improve your health, so get out there!).

Money: Money is another resource that is finite, so we pay attention to its use. I will not advocate spending more than you have or taking loans for any but a major purchase, like the house mentioned above.

Time: Time is perhaps the ultimate non-renewable resource, so we have to get the biggest impact for time invested. Many a project gets marked down on the analysis because it takes too long to occur regularly if you have jobs and family commitments -- it is not sustainable -- but I might include them because they are particularly pleasant or nice to do if you have downtime.

Natural Resources and Impact: This is always fighting territory. Is it more sustainable to deal with the global oil supply by getting off the grid and insisting on all solar or nothing, or should we drill, baby, drill? What is the cost/benefit analysis of different pest control options when weighing garden production versus potential run-off into the water table? What should you wear -- cotton, wool, hemp? -- and what is the impact on you and your community? You will have to weigh your options, as I do mine, and realize that responsible use of natural resources is a balancing act, not an all-or-nothing position. You will see that I lean toward using the resources we have on hand in a way that makes them last as long as possible and which has as much positive and as little negative impact on you, your family, and your community as possible, but you need to apply your values too.

Sustainable living is not a one-time decision, it is a continual process of trying, adjusting, and tweaking. No family's solution will be exactly the same as any other, and each will make decisions based on belief, philosophy, political perspective, research, and experience. To me, that's what makes it fun

On Not Paying for the Boring Stuff

I often make a bit of snarky fun of the financial-writer convention of using giving up a daily latte as a way to balance the budget. I have been guilty of doing this myself; as I also have suggested, coffee lovers will not want to be separated from their gourmet beverage of choice.

This is an example of one of my personal touchstones of sustainability: if you perceive a cut as a sacrifice, you will be less likely to follow through with it. Making a lifestyle change to sustainability is just like a diet; if you promise to give up your favorite cookies at New Year's, you will be off the wagon by February. But if you cut something from your diet you don't like anyway and perhaps substitute something healthy you love, it will become second nature.

Sustainability is the same way. If you are adopting this lifestyle to balance or cut back a budget, you will be tempted to start with the things you view as an extravagance, and cut there. Indeed, if you are facing five- or six-digit credit card debt, the loss of one or more household incomes, or bankruptcy and foreclosure, you probably will have to adopt a more monastic approach for a while.

However, if you are just looking to live a better life using fewer resources, I suggest you start by looking at the bill you hate most to pay, and make your initial changes there.

For me, it is the electric bill. Yes, I'm a big fan of summer air conditioning and running my various necessary appliances, but I absolutely hate the day the electric bill arrives. Somehow, it is boring, and I never really feel like I'm paying for something tangible, even if I am. So my first moves toward sustainable living addressed the electric bill. Easy changes I made included:

- Closing the window coverings on south-facing windows in the summer to keep out the heat from the sun.
- Hanging most laundry outside to dry, as soon as the air temperature was over 60. (I'm a wimp, but I just have a hard time heading outside to the line when it is chilly.)

- Making sure to bake more than one thing when I use the oven. If I do a roast, I will certainly bake bread and maybe a batch of cookies while it cooks.

- Only running a full dishwasher.

None of these were hard changes to make, and each one gave me a small feeling of control over that bill that I hated so much. And with the exception of hanging out the laundry (which did require purchase of a clothes line), every one of them was free and took very little time to execute. I just needed to think a little harder about the timing of some events.

As we move into our journey of sustainability, ask yourselves what you hate the most to waste: money, time, resources? Then ask yourself what aspect of your life bores or irritates you, and take your first sustainability steps there. How can you decrease a bill, produce less waste, or use less of a resource you value? Make it a challenge to yourself, almost like a game, and you will soon have a lifestyle.

Recharacterizing Waste

Every summer, my husband and I make our annual journey to the pick-your-own strawberry farm, then spent the rest of the day (and night) freezing strawberries and making jam and preserves. Preserves, by their nature, create a lot of liquid, so one year, after I canned the whole fruit preserves, I was left with a pot of strawberry syrup.

My first instinct was to throw it away; it was the by-product of preserves, not the product I was aiming for, so it must be waste. But then I thought better: this stuff wasn't waste. It was ice cream topping. It was coffee flavoring. It was a valuable product all its own. I canned two or three pints, and I enjoyed some over the winter in my coffee, a delicious abundance in a time of year that can feel very sparse and limited.

We need to do the same thing with all of our processes to lead a sustainable life. Rather than immediately consider something waste, we should ask ourselves what it becomes next. Holey towels become dust rags; old clothes become quilt pieces; poultry bones and pieces become stock. And yes, the leavings from canning can become flavorings, toppings, and other treats. In the process, our lives become filled with abundance, because we have limited our waste.

The Analysis

Fast: Changing your way of thinking may take time, but many forms of "waste" take less time to recharacterize than they do to dispose of. I can go through the hassle of taking fireplace ashes to my weekly trash can, or I can use them to line my compost bucket, reducing any food scrap odor and providing important nitrogen to my compost pile. The result is the best fertilizer on earth.

Cheap: Turning waste into abundance is always a financial win. It has the added benefit of reducing the amount of first-use "stuff" you have to buy, too. I'm certainly not buying strawberry coffee flavoring any more.

Good: A life with less waste and more abundance; quite good.

Front Yard Rebellion

Front yards are wonderful spaces; those of us lucky enough to own some land should be thankful. I realized this when engaging in a conversation about gardening with an urban dweller; when I started into my standard suburban apology for only having .71 acre on which to garden, he admitted to buying a house sitting on a tenth of an acre, almost solely because he could garden on it. I feel very blessed.

But often these front yards drive us far away from our neighbors, into our back yards. It is true of me: Sure, I trim the grass, prune the trees, and plant flowers out front, but the real fun -- the vegetable gardening -- goes on in the fenced in back yard. It is the same for many suburbanites: the front yard is for show, and the back yard is for living.

So I planned and executed a little suburban rebellion, by expanding my food operation into the front yard. Yes, I picked the prettiest plants -- the amethyst basil, the lime thyme, the feverfew -- for the front yard, but this ensures I will be kneeling out front, pulling weeds, and harvesting some of my herbs while the neighbors walk by.

Maybe they'll ask me for a sample. Maybe they'll be inspired to grow a food plant for the world to see, too. Wouldn't it be wonderful if we all did?

Knowing How

Mr. FC&G has a great story about an engineer who is called into the factory late one night to diagnose a problem with a machine that has stopped working, halting production. (After observing Mr. FC&G's work schedule, I might add that I am sure that it was late on a holiday or vacation evening, and that the engineer in question probably had to leave his wife to do this.)

He arrives and goes straight to the machine. He looks at the workings, takes a few readings, asks a few questions of the operators and the skilled trades folks, and then takes out a Sharpie and makes a big black X on the side.

"Open her up right there, and you'll see the problem," he says, giving directions about the part that needs replaced. He then packs up and, five minutes after he arrives, departs.

The next day he sends a bill for $5,000, and the client is irate. "What is this all about? You were only here for five minutes and made an X! I can't send this in for payment without some explanation of why it costs so much," the supervisor fumes. So the engineer writes a revised bill and sends it right over:

Making an X: $5
Knowing Where: $4,995

So, I hope you will see the connection when I point out that I thought of this when our air conditioner stopped working in 95 degree heat. Because my husband is, in fact, an electrical engineer, he went out, took a few readings, and diagnosed that we needed a new capacitor, which he ordered and installed. Total cost, $37. I'm sure I would have paid the HVAC service I use at least ten times that for the service call.

This is not to criticize the HVAC service or any other. (In fact, my HVAC guys have talked me through a few crises *gratis* before coming out and charging me, so kudos to them.) Instead, it is to point out that when you see the service charge on a bill, you are seeing the cost of "knowing how." And this should give you a good idea of the skills you may want to acquire. You don't have to learn electrical engineering, but can you learn enough basic wiring to install a new light fixture? (Obligatory warning: when messing with electricity, make sure you are doing it right.) Can you learn to change the oil in your car? Can you learn to make a meal so yummy you don't want to go out to eat as often? Can you sew on a button and mend a hem? Can you care for your body and reduce your health care costs?

Take a look at that service fee on your next bill, and see what skills you need to learn. Can you be the one that "knows how?"

Is Organization Frugal?

"That's so last season! I wouldn't be caught dead in it."

"Use it up, wear it out, make it do, or do without."

Somewhere between these two is where most frugalistas (and frugalistos) live. But it is easy to see how frugal living can tip the scale and send you right into accumulating too many things you will never use again.

For me, it was my clothes closet. I love getting new clothes, something that hasn't changed just because I want to live sustainably. However, a quick look at my closet one summer showed that I had gotten rid of very little since the early 1990s. Clothing was shoved, stacked, and stored in there: everything from current favorites to out-of-fashion but expensive pieces to cheapies that had seen better days. It was time to take action.

I was helped by two powerful forces. First is the recent proliferation of television shows about hoarding; after watching about two-thirds of an episode about these poor folks with disorders that resulted in the inability to throw things away, I invariably need to clean something out. More than one episode of such a show has ended with me holding a full trash bag.

The second, more powerful force is my wonderful Mom. She encouraged me to get rid of anything in my closet that I don't love and that doesn't make me feel good when I'm wearing it. No matter how expensive or how un-used (or, conversely, how loved-to-death), if it no longer works, it goes. When I needed a push forward, she would look at a piece of clothing with wide shoulder pads or an androgynous shape and parrot a commercial from a few years back: "So, where did you park your DeLorean?" No one wants to look like they are tooling around town with Marty McFly, so out the offending garment went.

This doesn't mean everything hit the trash. I tried to clean in a sustainable way, including:

- Items that were too worn to use became rags or quilt squares or hankies, as the fabric dictated. I tried to limit this category so I wasn't just moving stuff from my closet to another pile.

- Items that were still good but just didn't look good on me went to Goodwill. For example, I don't know how many mock turtlenecks I had to buy to learn the lesson that these shirts make me look like I have mono-bosom. Yuck.

- Items that no longer work but are more valuable as a garment than a rag also went to Goodwill. For example, wool jackets of a questionable cut were sent in the hopes that maybe they would be sold at deep discount to someone who needed the warmth more than the latest style. However, I didn't send anything obviously dated that was also super-cheap, like a cotton blouse with shoulder pads.

Is organization like this frugal and sustainable? I think so. Since the organization, I have been better able to find my favorite items, and I treat them better. Now that clothes have room to breathe, I am less likely to pull something out of the closet only to find that it needs ironed before wearing. I have also better been able to resist buying a new item because I didn't remember that I had one similar tucked away on the shelf.

The organization has also carried over into my shopping. Now, when I shop, I ask myself if I really love something, if it will look good on me, if it will make me feel good about myself. If it is just OK or a "like not love," I put it back on the rack. Someone else who loves the item can give it a home and "use it up, wear it out." I will do likewise with my favorites before I shop for new ones. I think that's sustainable.

The Value of Stretching

Stretching is something of a lost art. Your grandmother or great-grandmother did it during the Depression and WWII, taking a little bit of rationed foodstuffs and turning it into enough food to feed a family. In fact, home cooks throughout history have stretched their food -- making do with the scarce or expensive items and adding in cheaper or in-season items to add bulk, volume, taste, or nutrition. Cookbooks from most eras explicitly or implicitly refer to stretching; it is only modern cookbooks that seem to imply that you can't make dinner unless you have the exact quantities asked for, down to the last bay leaf and quarter teaspoon of lemon zest.

Some of my favorite stretching tips:

To Stretch Meat

- Meat is the most often stretched foodstuff, because of scarcity in earlier eras and expense in all eras. The best way to stretch meat is grind it up: buy a less expensive cut and grind it, or buy pre-ground chuck, turkey, or the like. Stretch by adding approximately one egg per pound of ground meat and up to a cup of oatmeal, bread crumbs, rice, or cracker crumbs. Behold, meatloaf! Meat balls! Just season according to your recipe. This is the stretching tip you most likely remember from your granny, and it is the one you are most likely to still use, even if you don't think of it as stretching.

- Slice your meat. With a better cut of meat, prepare it and then slice it and use it as a garnish on pasta, rice, or salads. You will want less meat when it visually takes up more room, and this also means fewer calories in your diet.

- Use the scraps. We keep a "stock bucket" in our freezer to collect trimmings and bones. When it is full, I make stock and use that for a hearty soup.

- Make a casserole from leftovers. If you have a few trimmings from a roast or even a few hot dogs from your last cook out, you can add them to a casserole for a little extra protein and a meal with less meat.

To Stretch Carbohydrates

- Carbs, like pasta, rice, or bread, are usually the thing we use to stretch. However, in some seasons, they are the most expensive item on a very economical table. When the garden is in full swing, suddenly that $1 box of pasta is your big expense for the meal.

- Stretch pizza crust and most baked goods by adding shredded zucchini. I like to take a Jiffy boxed pizza crust and add about a cup of shredded zucchini (about one medium) and decrease the amount of water called for. Add a little extra flour if the dough seems watery. Often, this makes a small box of pizza crust mix become enough for two pizzas.

- Likewise, put a shredded zucchini in your next batch of bread and decrease the liquid a bit. You will get more bread, and you have found a way to get rid of a zucchini and add some nutrition to your diet.

To Stretch Dairy

- Dairy is expensive, especially if you want hormone-free or organic varieties.

- Make yogurt. Yogurt can take the place of many sauces, and it becomes a good way to get calcium without having to drink a lot of milk. While an ounce of milk makes an ounce of yogurt, so no real change in volume, you tend to be happy with four to six ounces of yogurt and some fruit instead of an eight ounce glass of milk.

- Buy stronger flavored cheeses. That way, you will use less and still be satisfied. Mizithra, although a little hard to find and a bit expensive, adds a lot of flavor to pasta with a just a little bit of grated cheese.

- Use cheese as a garnish on veggies, not as a main ingredient.

Recapturing Heat

Here are five ways to make your house toastier without spending any extra money:

1. Reset your ceiling fans. This was once a matter of great debate between my father and I, so let me say for the record that your fan should be set with the downward edge of the blade going forward, which is usually clockwise. Many fans will settle the debate for you by putting "winter" and "summer" on the switch. This pushes the warm air at the ceiling downward, which keeps the living area of the room warmer. We don't have ceiling fans at Casa FC&G other than in the sunroom, but they do make a difference.

2. Stop the dishwasher mid-dry-cycle: This is one of my favorite tips. I set the dishwasher to do a dry cycle as part of the normal wash, then stop it midway through and open the dishwasher door. The dishes are already dry and as sterilized as they are going to get, and all that lovely steam and heat comes out and fills the kitchen.

3. Leave the clothes dryer open a minute or two: If you like to fold your clothes in the laundry room, leave the dryer door open while you do it. The heat inside the dryer drum will come out into the room. Be careful, because depending on how well your dryer is vented to the outside and how secure the baffles are, you can quickly get outside cold air. But that initial burst of warmth is wonderful.

4. Leave the pot on the stove: If you boil pasta or potatoes, lift the food out with a strainer or slotted spoon and leave the boiling pot on the stove (with the burner off) while you eat. The heat will escape into the room. This is also a great excuse for making stock during the winter.

5. Open the oven door: My all-time favorite. When you do you regularly-scheduled baking, open the oven door when you are done to get a burst of 350 degree air coming into your kitchen.

The Analysis

Fast: None of these ideas should take more than a few seconds to implement. Would I steer you into a long, drawn-out project?

Cheap: You probably won't notice a huge difference in your heat bills, but every degree counts in the winter.

Good: Keeping warm while saving money is what we are all about!

Four Reasons to Shop Locally for the Holidays

1. Shopping local is sustainable: Much of this book focuses on things you can do to be self-sufficient, but no person is an island. We cannot live entirely alone; human beings live in communities. I suggest you use your money to support your neighbors' work, in the process keeping the money in your local community. Eventually, it will come back to you. That is a sustainable system.

Gift idea: Rather than ordering gift baskets of food from large distribution organizations or those mall kiosks, go to the winter farmers' market and buy local jams, preserves, sausages, and cheese, and put those all in a pretty container. Even if you are carrying the goodies a long way to Grandma's house, the purchases will support your community, and you are sure to have a one-of-a-kind gift.

2. Shopping local is economically viable: One way to support your community is to exchange your skill for someone else's. Yes, that sometimes means barter, but primarily, we use money as an intermediary in the process. So, you trade your skill as a computer programmer or a welder or a teacher for money, and then you can trade that for someone else's product. I suggest you keep that money and that effort in your own community by buying as much as possible from local providers. If you are in an area such as mine, which is still feeling the impact of the recession, those dollars kept at home will do far more good than they would if they took an expensive trip to a corporate HQ.

Gift idea: Rather than buying a mass-produced item, consider supporting an artisan who is now making a living off of his or her skill. A local woodworker, for example, could potentially create anything from a set of coasters to a fabulous Adirondack chair, and you are sure that you are spending your money with someone in your community while you give an interesting gift.

3. Shopping local is political: This is not a political book; I don't care if my readers vote or think the way I do. However, I do hope my readers are voting with their dollars (or yen or euros) by supporting businesses that behave the way they believe is responsible. Have you

ever tried to trace the supply chain for a product from a large conglomerate? Physical supplies come from all over the globe, as do administrative supports and marketing. With your local businesses, your artisan is often the same one standing behind the counter, and that person can tell you in detail where the supplies came from and how the product was made. If you agree that the person behaved responsibly and ethically, then your money is a vote to support continuation of that behavior.

Gift idea: There are fewer worries about poor workplace conditions or questionable executive behavior when you buy local. Quiz your local merchant about the supply and production chain when purchasing. Try to find local substitutes for things you might otherwise buy from a faceless conglomerate, like knitwear from a local knitter who uses natural fiber yarns.

4. Shopping local is environmental: OK, not always. But if you want raw honey or a product made without latex or a gift that uses as many upcycled items as possible, your best bet is the local provider. If the large conglomerates have economies of scale on their side, then the small local provider has the advantage of overseeing the process in minute detail. This means you can use your purchase to support a business that protects the environment in a way that you believe is effective.

Gift idea: Think about bypassing the cookie-cutter gifts in favor of unique items that fit your sustainable beliefs. There are many artisans in your community that work with upcycled items and create beautiful jewelry and household decorations that involve very little new raw material.

Do What You Would Anyway: Secrets of a Very Part-Time Job

It is the holiday season, which means that the sustainability and frugality blogosphere is full of discussions of whether to tighten our belts or find ways to earn more money for gift-giving. This is, of course, an individual choice. And while I'm never going to tell you to live outside your means, there are times (holidays and vacations come to mind) when we all would like to extend our means just a little bit.

That means more money.

Here at FC&G, we spend most of our time trying to live within the resources that we have. Often that is money, but it is often also resources like food or energy or time. But we also talk about extending those resources, such as when we grow more veggies in a small space. And I want to talk today about my theory on earning more money the FC&G way.

As you all know, Mr. FC&G and I run Carrot Creations, our shop dedicated to providing sustainable living gear that we hand-make. As you also know, I have a full-time job with Hilltop Communications and the second-shift job at the college. Mr. FC&G is similarly over-extended. About the last thing we need is another job, but I love Carrot Creations.

Last week, the store made its 52nd sale for the year (not all of them appear on the Etsy tally, if you are checking up on me, because we sell face-to-face too), which averages one sale a week. Although many people sell much more, I am very happy with this, and here are some of my keys to success of a very-part-time (VPT) money making endeavor:

Make it something you would do anyway: I love to crochet, knit, and sew fleece. I would do it regardless of whether it would sell. I have made many dozen pairs of fleece socks for myself, Mr. FC&G, and family. Having a way to sell these items gives me an excuse to make them without feeling guilty that I'm just buying lots of fleece and yarn to make items we don't really need. The work doesn't feel like a job, someone else gets cozy feet and lower heating bills, and I make a couple of bucks. It feels like a win-win.

Make it scalable: Your VPT money maker can't hold you down, or it destroys your quality of life. If I have a lull in either my writing work or the second shift, I can make socks and cowls to my heart's content and have them ready for future sales. If I am swamped, I can ignore the production side and just ship orders. If I'm on vacation, I can close the store. Carrot Creations doesn't hamper our lifestyle.

If making hand-made items isn't your thing, remember that there are a number of scalable and temporary part-time jobs out there. More than once, I have had part-time jobs that involved subbing for regular staff, so the organization would call me when needed and I could say yes or no to the shift according to my own schedule. I have also long intended to one year try a seasonal job, like a Christmas retail job or an Easter ham store job. Some people regularly work the polls on election day and otherwise take one-day jobs. If you look, these little jobs are out there.

Make it part of your dream: Yes, many of us occasionally hit a point at which all income, even little extras, needs to be earmarked for living expenses. But if yours doesn't, don't be afraid to tie your efforts with your VPT job to a dream. Put the profits in a vacation fund, a home-improvement fund, or even your garden seed fund. It is so much fun to get to buy one of these treats without dipping into your regular income, and it makes it that much more enjoyable to work your VPT job.

Failure to Forage

When it comes to sustainable living projects, I'm a bit like an eight-year-old on Christmas morning when I discover one I haven't tried before. I have salivated over DIY solar collectors for south-facing windows, pondered backyard chickens, and calculated how much herb gardening I can sneak into the front yard under the guise of decorative plants. So naturally, when the *Old Farmer's Almanac* posted a link to Facebook detailing how to process acorns to make acorn meal, I was irrationally excited.

"I have oak trees; there's food out there for the taking!" I thought, grabbing a bowl and heading to the side yard. In no time, I had a heaping bowlful, which I placed in a sunny spot in the nearly-completed sunroom for drying while I took time to investigate my next steps.

Now, I should note that our suburban back yard is like no other I've ever experienced. In spite of living on a corner lot near a fairly busy road, the fenced back yard typically looks like a Disney film on crack. At any given time, you have no problem locating squirrels, chipmunks, and rabbits -- and most of them are completely unfazed by humans. One spring -- I swear I'm not making this up -- I saw a mother rabbit lead three young bunnies to the edge of the garden fence and practically show them how to crawl through the spaces. Another year -- and I'm not making this up either, nor was I on large doses of cold medicine at the time -- I watched a pair of squirrels chase one another across our fence, only to take a flying leap to land on our window awning. They did this repeatedly for a good 15 minutes. Our creatures are insane, and they seem to view me more as pest than predator.

So, it should not have surprised me when I went out to the sunroom and found two acorns, well-nibbled, in the corner of the room. I assumed I had dropped them, and I cleaned them up. The next day, I went out to find the opposite corner now totally filled with shredded acorns and discarded shells, along with a very much emptied bowl of acorns.

Long story short, I stormed out to the compost in my homemade fleece socks (too mad to put on flip flops) and got rid of my sustainable acorns, then my poor husband spent the evening taping any likely cracks in the house that might be an entry point for nefarious chipmunks who think I have put out a buffet for them.

I don't think we'll be living on acorn meal any time soon.

Jennifer Patterson Lorenzetti

3 Gardening

Gardening has been a passion of mine since I was a little girl. My maternal grandparents owned a farm, and I remember going to pick strawberries with my grandmother. There is nothing so sweet as a strawberry fresh from the vine, still warmed by the sun.

The moment I could convince my parents to till up some land, I had a garden. I grew everything I could think of, and my great-aunt taught me how to pickle cucumbers and can tomatoes. I still think of her and of my grandmother every time gardening season comes around.

Gardening is, to me, the quintessential sustainability activity. It gives you control over the quality of your food while also allowing you to eat as locally as possible – there are few things more local than a tomato that came from your back yard. You control the presence or absence of chemicals, the fertilizers, and how the plants are treated.

Most important, however, is that you get to see a living thing grow under your hands to ultimately support your well-being. It's a magic things, seeing a seedling that you nursed under a grow light in March suddenly giving you dinners-full of produce in August.

Whether you have a sunny windowsill or a fertile "back 40," I hope you'll join me in growing some of your own food.

Starting Pepper Seeds Under a Grow Light

I typically start my pepper seeds on Groundhog Day; by Valentine's Day, I have a full tray of little seedlings, each with their bright green first pair of leaves unfolded to the light. So, it is time to give them something to reach for.

Many seed-starting handbooks (and virtually all gardening catalogs) will start you salivating over "seedling condominiums," these sets of shelves with adjustable banks of grow lights suspended overhead. They are lovely, and they will set you back somewhere around $200-$300. If you are going into commercial seedling production, this may be a reasonable capital expenditure. I, however, just want a nice cheap supply of peppers and salsa.

So, I took an old desk lamp, and I inserted a $3 grow bulb in it. The bulb will provide the correct spectrum of light for the peppers to grow, and you are only out the cost of the bulb. (Sorry, a traditional fluorescent or incandescent bulb won't do it, because it won't throw the correct parts of the light spectrum for the plants. Opinions are mixed on this score, and a traditional fluorescent is better than nothing, but I find my seeds perform better under a dedicated grow bulb.)

The drawback of this approach is that you will need to shift the light during the day so each pot of seedlings gets direct light. They like to have at least 14 hours of light, so it helps to have your seedlings in a high-traffic area (mine are in the kitchen) so you will nudge the light whenever you pass. However, this system has worked very well for me for years.

We don't need to do anything else to the peppers until we see a first set of "true" leaves. Until then, just turn that light on in the morning and let them grow!

The Analysis

Fast: You can pick up a grow bulb at any hardware store or greenhouse, or most grocers. I know you have an old desk lamp sitting around, or some other lamp with a goose-type neck that will shine down on your peppers.

Cheap: I usually purchase one grow bulb a year at about $3. This ultimately becomes part of an array of lights and windows for seedling growth, so it works out to be a good deal, and much better than those seedling condos.

Good: Peppers are still the goal here, and we're one step closer to salsa!

Compost Q&A

For me, the epitome of "Fast, Cheap, and Good" might be composting. It is quick and easy to toss your organic waste into a compost pile, it certainly costs nothing, and it keeps waste out of the landfills while generating beautiful humus for your garden.

For the novice composter, however, composting appears to be a difficult chore. Our culture simply doesn't teach us to compost, and marketers have rushed into the void with tons of products meant to "get you started." Instead, let's start with some common questions from composting novices:

Is composting difficult?
No. Remember, much of human history has been lived without a weekly trash pick-up. Communities regularly put their waste into piles; archeologists love this kind of thing. What we are going to do is use a natural decomposition process to take care of organic waste, which will result in fewer beads and pottery shards for future archeologists, but might keep the planet around long enough for future excavations.

Does compost smell bad?
Yes and no. Part of the misunderstanding about compost comes from the fact that we use the word "compost" to mean three separate phases of the project. Let me break these down and give each its own term:

"Raw compost" is your table scraps, egg shells, and the like. If you let this sit around in your compost container in the house, it will indeed mold and smell bad. A little fireplace wood ash in the bottom of your container will control the odor, but it really needs to go out on the pile to start breaking down.

"Working compost" is the material in your pile. This is the stuff from your household compost bucket, plus dirt, grass clippings, fallen leaves, and the like. Earthworms and certain soil bacteria love this, and as they munch away, they assist the process of decomposition. If your compost pile smells, it is probably because you have too much "green matter" (generally from raw compost) and too little "brown matter" (like leaves, grass, and dirt). If your working compost pile smells, you need to stir it with a pitchfork and add a little brown matter to the top. Easy.

"Finished compost" is humus, the dark brown dirt that can be used as potting soil or as garden fertilizer. One of the ways you know it is finished is by the smell -- it smells of life, freshness, and spring. It is truly one of my favorite scents.

Do I need an expensive container?
No. Garden retailers have devised a number of products for compost creation, most of which are unnecessary. One of these is the rotating plastic drum that is supposed to generate finished compost in two to six weeks. Who needs their compost that fast? A large-scale gardener might, but then that person will need a lot more finished compost than can be created in that drum.

There is one circumstance in which a commercial compost drum might be useful: If you are composting in an urban environment or one in which you have absolutely no land (like an apartment or a condo with restrictive common space regulations), you may only be able to compost in a container. Otherwise, you should try to put your compost in contact with the ground.

Do I need compost additives?
Again, compost additives, like live earthworms and bacteria innoculant, are useful only for container composting. Even then, a few shovels of "live" dirt (that is, not the sterilized stuff sold as potting soil) and a few earthworms (which I would be tempted to buy cheap at a bait shop) will do the trick.

Are my neighbors going to complain?
If you are worried about the neighbors, your job is either to educate them or to make sure they never know you are composting. If you choose the latter, you may want to enclose your pile in a frame made of picket fence panels rather than the chicken wire that folks like me use. You can use the same set of construction instructions one would use to make an enclosure for an air conditioner compressor, only be

sure to use fence panels with openings that will let in rain and air. Monitor your pile closely for any odor that indicates you need more brown matter, and your neighbors shouldn't even know unless they come over and lift the lid.

Will I attract critters?

I will confess that I sometimes leave strawberry trimmings on the top of the pile to feed the rabbits that inhabit my property. (Then I complain mightily a month later when they have stayed around to eat my tomatoes.) Small herbivores shouldn't be much of a concern for you, but if you are concerned about larger animals, be certain that you always mix the raw compost into the working pile very well.

More Veggies in Less Space: The Cucumber Trellis

Every year, Mr. FC&G and I budget for a garden improvement or two. In this way, our vegetable production space has grown from a small, unfenced patch that we had when we first moved to our "microfarm" to a large fenced space, supported by a container garden and five ancillary spaces and raised beds.

One year, we invested in cucumber trellises, simply one of the best purchases we have made. Ours are from Gardener's Supply, but you could fairly easily make your own; they are basically a trellis in front supported by legs in the bag and held in the ground with garden staples (not included). It would be a pretty easy project.

The cucumber trellis (it also works well for peas, beans, and other vining veggies) allows the cucumber vines to grow up the front, keeping the majority of the fruit off the ground, safe from critters and decomposition. It also allows the fruit to hang down and grow straight, which means cucumbers are easier to fit in pickle jars. Because the vines are held up off the ground with good air circulation, they are less likely to contract mildews that will kill the plant, and if they do, they do a better job of fighting it off.

It is hard to quantify vegetable production year to year, but with the trellis I have cucumbers for about a month longer than I usually do without, and I believe I have better production overall. A valuable bonus is that the vines crawling up the trellis create a shaded spot underneath (if you have positioned the trellis correctly), so you can grow lettuces and cool season small crops underneath even in the hot weather, further increasing your yield.

I left the trellises out in the garden all winter, and they weathered beautifully. At about $60 for two (including shipping), depending on your love of cucumbers and pickles, I estimate these could pay for themselves in two or three years.

Sustainable Tool: The Broadfork

"Oh, I knew I never should have let you read those *Little House on the Prairie* books," my mom laughed when I posted a picture to Facebook of FC&G's household's new broadfork.

A broadfork is kind of a pitchfork on steroids. It features a row of sturdy, curved tines about 18 inches long attached to a crossbar. Double handles allow you to use both hands on the tool easily.

The beauty of this is that one can jam those tines in the ground, then pull back on the handles and not so much flip the soil as loosen it. This is instrumental since we have started "lasagna gardening," a strategy in which you do not plow/rototill your soil so that you keep the various strata intact instead of destroying the work your beneficial flora and fauna have done to your soil over the year. This keeps down the presence of annoying insects and diseases.

You do this by continually mulching the soil, allowing the mulch to compost in situ. I like to think of lasagna gardening as the "I hate to rototill" method. If you keep mulching through summer, it keeps the weeds under control too.

In any event, if you practice lasagna gardening, you need to loosen that soil periodically, and this is what the broadfork is for. It is fun to use, although my husband is more effective at it than me. It is a great workout, as you might imagine, and it is certainly going to outlast a gas-powered rototiller, not to mention have a much smaller impact on the environment. I love my broadfork, and I think Pa Ingalls might have been proud.

The Analysis

Fast: The broadfork does a quicker job of "tilling" the garden than would a rototiller, once you factor in the inevitable spring ritual of calling every hardware store in the area, going to rent one, trying to make sure you have the proper fuel, letting it jerk you around the garden for a couple of hours, and then cleaning it for the return.

Cheap: This was $99 plus shipping from Lehman's, my favorite store for sustainable stuff. The shipping was pretty expensive (about $25) as you might expect. However, we have a theory around here that sometimes it is better to invest in a really good tool rather than simply having the money in the bank. Preparedness and the ability to do a good job are a kind of savings, too.

Good: Broadforking my garden is better for the health of my soil and for the size of my waistline. Sustainable tool win!

Let's Talk About (Squash) Sex

One of the most frequent things I am asked, when conversations turn to the garden, is how I know whether the blossoms on my pumpkins, zucchini, and butternut squashes are male or female. And I just love to talk about (squash) sex!

Now, this is still a PG-rated book, so I'm not using this as a euphemism, for all of you who are taking "hide the zucchini" a little too literally. No, I mean the fact that not all squash blossoms are created equal. There are males and females, and, like all organisms with two sexes, you need both to get a baby. In this case we want our baby to be a bouncing one pound zucchini or five pound pie pumpkin, so it helps to know if your squash plants are setting up the proper conditions for procreation.

Consider the male blossom, on which the flower is lifted up on a fairly thin stem. This stem will never produce a fruit; its purpose is to get that delicious pollen out for the bees to pick up and deliver to female flowers. You can often see the male flowers bloom in the mornings because they are so much more apparent than the females. It is also typical for a squash plant to put out many males before it produces any females, so the bees get used to where to go to get their pollen. Some years, I have had plants with only males, and then I did not get any squash.

On a female, the fruit sits behind the blossom and waits for the blossom to be fertilized. If it is not, it will yellow, dry, and fall off. If it does, you can see it start to plump up, and it looks green and healthy when the blossom falls off. You will know the females straight away because those are the blossoms you see that have a "little squash" on them.

So now you know! If this is new information to you, remember that you are never too old to keep learning about sex!

4 Recipes

As I mentioned in the introduction, the earliest household guides were recipe books with the addition of "household helps" geared toward helping the homemaker run her domain. Typically, the recipes took up most of the book, with the other sections complementing the recipe section. I hope I've replicated that here.

These recipes are favorites in our house, and they range from beverages to main dishes. Some are incredibly local and sustainable, and some are just a small improvement over what you might buy in a store or restaurant. Some are ultra-cheap, and some are just somewhat less expensive than an upscale version. But, since we tend to eat two to three meals a day, every day, every little bit we save or improve adds up quickly!

Poor Man's Latte

Some days, I feel kind of sorry for Starbucks. After all, they built a business by selling an experience: for a few minutes every morning, you could go somewhere and have things just as you like them. If you want a triple shot of espresso, extra raspberry syrup, but no whipped cream, you just tell the barista, preferably speaking that special little code that puts the ingredients in just the right order. Part quirky hangout, part predictable chain, part special club, Starbucks was never really about the coffee.

But the 2008 recession hit, and soon frugality and finance writers made a great deal of hay out of what you could save by giving up that daily latte. I think I've been guilty of that one at least once myself. (If you are curious, giving up a $3.50 latte every work day for a year, minus two weeks' vacation, will save you $875.) I'll bet the PR department at Starbucks groans every time they read a frugality article, because they know they will be the first suggestion for a cut.

Working at home is a great deterrent to getting a daily coffee at a coffee house, but one thing will send me cruising back, at least temporarily, into the arms of Seattle's best-known export: the annual arrival of Pumpkin Spice Latte, and its cousin, Gingerbread Latte. Good heavens, these things are like drinking cookies!

In an effort to provide the same experience for less cost, I experimented, and I have come up with my "Poor Man's Latte." Coffee snobs will turn up their noses, but this recipe seems to provide just the right hint of extravagance without the high price. You will need:

1 large mug coffee
1 scant spoonful instant pudding mix (Sometimes, a pumpkin flavor is available; check around Thanksgiving for seasonal flavors and stock up.)
1 scant spoonful honey (I buy raw honey from a local provider; see caution below.)

That's it! The pudding mix gives a bit of that latte mouthfeel to the coffee, so you may need less milk than you usually use. You should be able to satisfy your latte cravings for significantly less than $1 a mug (depending on local honey costs and whether you also want a splash of milk), counting coffee, flavoring, and water costs.

Caution

Raw honey has not been pasteurized, so you should not feed it to anyone you think is immuno-compromised. And, of course, never give honey to an infant under the age of one, because their immune systems are not mature enough to handle the risk of ingesting trace amounts of botulism spores. Older than that, and we build up our immunity to these spores and can handle them just fine if our immune systems are healthy.

The Assessment:

Fast: Yep. Yes, it takes an extra moment to add in the flavorings to your coffee, but it sure takes less time than standing in line in a coffee house.

Cheap: Yep. The flavoring mix is only pennies per cup.

Good: Your call. I have a sweet tooth, and I'm not much of a coffee snob, so I'm not going to get worked up about masking the refined flavors of the beans or some such. If brewing fine coffee is one of your passions, you won't be making your budget cuts in this area. Then again, if that is the case, you are probably already grinding beans and brewing at home anyway, and you never set foot in a chain coffee house.

Jen's Perfect Mojito

A mojito is, at its most basic, a rum and club soda concoction flavored with mint and lime. Occasionally, it will contain lime juice and cane sugar or syrup. In our travels, we have discovered that the farther south one travels, the more likely one is to get a very dry mojito, without juice or sweetener. In Maryland, we had some delicious mojitos that were more like really sweet rum soda pop than anything else; hit the Southernmost key in the union, and a mojito is very likely to be more along the lines of a gin and tonic, with the garnishes flavoring the mix as they sit and combine.

With much experimentation for the benefit of you, my dear reader, I believe I have come upon the Perfect Mojito. You will need:

2 oz. white rum (I prefer Ten Cane)
2 oz. club soda
2 oz. lime juice (look for Nellie and Joe's Key West Lime Juice)
2 oz. simple syrup (Make your own: it is a 1:1 combo of cane sugar and water. Heat until combined and keep a jar in the fridge.)
1 lime (Key limes are best, but you can use Persian limes in a pinch.)
2 sprigs mojito mint (Grow your own, or use spearmint if you must.)

In a rocks glass, muddle the lime (cut in half and retain a slice for garnish) and one sprig of the mojito mint. You need to muddle, or crush, these elements to release the oils from the lime skin and the flavor of the mint. Mojito mint is a more robust, less sweet Cuban mint that gives a more authentic flavor.

Add the rum, lime juice, simple syrup, and club soda, and mix. Garnish with the remaining lime wedge and sprig of mint.

Enjoy, and dream of the tropics!

The Analysis

Fast: If you have all your inputs in one place, you should be able to mix this pretty quickly. If you need to make mojitos for a party, cut your limes ahead of time and keep your mint sprigs in a glass of water. Mix the club soda, lime juice, and simple syrup ahead of time in a pitcher, then add the rum individually to the cocktails.

Cheap: Um, no. A bottle of Ten Cane is north of $35.00 around here, and this is before you buy the premium lime juice and start growing your own mint. The cocktail above is easily $3-4 in ingredients, which is about half the price for which you can get them in local restaurants and is far less than the $10-12 for a mojito in Key West, which is usually made with far-cheaper Bacardi or Mount Gay rum. There is, however, that beach element that makes it worthwhile. However, for those of us trapped north of Cayo Hueso, I am not going to recommend any but the finest mojito I know how to mix!

Good: Yes. Oh, yes.

Mr. FC&G's Hot Toddy

Well, it was inevitable. I caught Mr. FC&G's cold. It makes sense; we share everything, and that includes the germs.

Luckily, Mr. FC&G was on the mend by the time I caught it, and he was ready with warm "knee thingies" (heat wraps) in the bed and multiple birthday cakes, since I got sick on my birthday and consequently couldn't eat my cake as fast as he could "help" me. (Gotta love a man that keeps making cake to be sure that you are satisfied!) And, best of all, he made hot toddies.

I don't know what it was about this simple recipe, but every time he made me a toddy, I felt better and better. I think we have decided to keep making and drinking toddies all winter, just to be sure we stay in tip-top health.

Mr. FC&G's Hot Toddy
1 mug herbal tea (I like chai tea for this)
raw honey to taste
scant 1/2 shot whiskey

Mix all ingredients in a mug and drink while hot. Repeat as needed.

The Analysis

Fast: This takes no longer to make than a mug of tea, so pretty speedy.

Cheap: Frankly, I have no idea if this is cheaper than Nyquil or a similar over the counter medicine. I do know that it worked better for me than do most of those cold meds.

Good: I felt so much better after each of these toddies, all warm and pretty energetic. They certainly have gotten me through the worst of a cold, and that counts for a lot.

Simple Syrup

So, one day I was in a bar (and you don't know how long I've waited to start a sustainable living post that way...), and I asked the bartender for a mojito. The establishment was new, and it was still stocking up, and the bartender allowed as how she had no simple syrup and would have to "get some."

Friends, one does not buy simple syrup. You know why? Take a gander at a search for "simple syrup" on Amazon. When I quoted this in 2011, you would pay $31.13 plus shipping for four bottles of simple syrup, each just over a quart.

If I ever catch any of you spending $32 to buy a gallon of simple syrup, I am coming to your house and not leaving until you are rebatching your soap, making your own laundry detergent, and starting a compost pile.

For those of you planning to make cocktails, you need to know this: Simple syrup is **simple.** It is equal parts sugar and water. Just take your granulated cane sugar (I usually use a cup) and put it in a small sauce pan with an equal amount (a cup) of water. Heat on low until the sugar dissolves, and then pop it in the fridge. Bingo. You have enough simple syrup to get you through a few cocktails or a pitcher of mojitos, for pennies.

I mean, I get it: sometimes you buy stuff to stock your bar. If you never make your own aromatic bitters (which you totally can, but since you use two drops of the stuff at a time, a store-bought bottle should last a decade anyway), you will still have your sustainability merit badge from me. But you use simple syrup by the shot and jigger-full, and there is no reason to waste money on something you can make while you are slicing your limes.

The Analysis

Fast: Literally, simple syrup takes 2 minutes to make.

Cheap: Pennies, I tell you. What does a bag of sugar even cost these days? A few bucks for 4 pounds of cane sugar, and that would make a few gallons of simple syrup. Never pay $32 a gallon!!

Good: Saving your money for the expensive rum is always a better deal when stocking the bar.

Rescuing the Bread Machine: Four Ingredient French Bread

Here's a quickie project that can net big financial returns (on a percentage basis, anyway): Four Ingredient French Bread.

I can hear the groans. If you aren't making your own bread already, you are no doubt deterred by the whole knead-and-rise cycle, and I don't blame you. I absolutely hate the process of turning the dough out onto the counter to knead it at least twice per loaf, and I really hate cleaning the flour up off the counter or cutting board or whatever I decided to use. Somehow, this bit of the process always makes me feel that I'm tied to my kitchen for the entire day. ("Nope, sorry, you'll have to go to the movies without me; it's baking day!")

Enter the bread machine. Remember that Christmas, probably about 20 years ago at this point, that everyone got their bread machines? I know your family had one: the year that every present under the tree seemed to be the same large, heavy cube, and everyone took turns exclaiming in glee over their new toy that would ensure fresh baked bread every day.

Wrong. The thing is, most of those bread machine recipes turned out to be very complex (I remember buying a huge box of powdered milk, because my machine required something like a tablespoon per loaf of white bread. Good thing that stuff is shelf stable.). If you did manage to hang in, you got one of those oddly crispy-all-around square loaves with the little divot in the bottom where the mixing paddle sat. No thanks.

But now, I want you to go into the attic or the basement, and retrieve that bread machine. If you sold yours, I'm sure your mom, your brother, or your Aunt Gertrude isn't as organized as you, so borrow theirs. And then, find the "dough" cycle.

Most of these machines have an option in which you can use them to just mix and knead the dough and let it rise. If yours doesn't, you can still complete this recipe; just use the "white" or "light" bread cycle, and take the dough out before the baking cycle begins. You will need:

3 cups white flour
1 cup water (plus or minus a tablespoon or two, depending on the humidity in your house)
1 T. bread machine (fast acting) yeast
1 t. salt

That's it. Now throw all that in the machine's hopper, set it for "dough," and walk away.

My dough cycle runs for an hour and 30 minutes. Sometime at about the halfway point, once I know the ingredients have been through the mix cycle and at least one rise, I take the dough out and put it in a greased bread pan or on a cookie sheet if I want more of a long, thin loaf. Then I let the dough rise for the final time.

Sometime, I'm working and I completely forget about the bread, so it makes it through both rises in the machine and just sits there. Big deal (unless you don't have the dough cycle -- then set yourself an egg timer so you don't forget to do something to the dough before it bakes). If I forget it, I just let it raise a third time in the baking vessel of choice.

When the bread has roughly doubled in size, pop it in a 350 degree oven for 35 minutes, take it out, and enjoy. If it is winter, don't forget to prop that oven door open while it cools off to let the heat escape into the house!

Variations
There are a couple of easy variations to this recipe that will increase the health value:

- Experiment with specialty flours. Right now, I like a mix of one cup each of white flour, light whole wheat flour, and oat flour. This increases the whole grain content of the bread.
- Add one tablespoon of flax seeds to increase the omega-3 fatty acid content. They make a nice little crunch (kind of like the caraway seeds in rye), and the extra omega-3s help ward off depression, which is no joke around here when the days are so short and the sunlight so precious.

- If you make your own cheese, substitute one cup of the remaining whey for the water to increase the protein and use up more of that valuable and often-wasted whey.

The Analysis

Fast: Yep. I timed this one out, and the entire process takes 2:12 with two rises of the bread. Your involvement is 12 minutes: I gave you a minute for each of the ingredients, a minute or two to take the bread out of the machine and put it in the baking vessel, and a minute to take it out of the oven. I even gave you a minute to dust your bread machine. If you have to venture into the attic or go to Aunt Gertrude's, you are going to have to view that as a sunk cost.

Cheap: Again, yep. Depending on ingredient cost, you should be able to bake a loaf of the basic four ingredient bread for under $1, which is hard to beat at the store. If you use one of the variations, the loaf will cost somewhat more, but then you would have to compare your product to the price of specialty breads, and you will still come out ahead. Plus, you know that your bread has no preservatives and no high fructose corn syrup.

Good: Have you tasted homemade bread? Or smelled it baking? This loaf wins this contest hands down. You know exactly what you put in it, so you know exactly what is entering your body and exiting your pocketbook.

Homemade Croutons

Isn't it funny how there are some categories of items that you don't think of making for yourself? This occurred to me as I prepared Easter dinner; while I expect to grow my own greens and veggies, sometimes I forget that things like salad dressings and croutons are also easy to make in a way that is fast, cheap, and good.

So, one Easter I made my own croutons. The crouton project is as easy as can be, and it is a super-cheap way to create really high-quality croutons for your salad.

First, I baked a loaf of Four Ingredient French Bread, altering the flour mix to 2 cups of white and 1 cup of whole wheat. Most recipes for croutons will tell you to use stale bread, but if I wait for a loaf of stale homemade bread around this house, I'll never have croutons!

I cut the loaf into thick slices and then 1-inch cubes. I tossed the cubes in butter, sprinkled with salt, pepper, and dried basil from the garden (you could use oregano, sage, or many others, depending on what flavor you want for your salad). And then I baked in a 350 degree oven until toasty-crisp on the outside and still a bit soft on the inside.

On our Caesar salad, they looked pretty and tasted wonderful. I'll be making my own from now on.

The Analysis

Fast: Yes, this took more time than buying a package of those powdery, preservative-filled things from the store. But I have bread-baking down to a science, and I baked the croutons while something else was in the oven, so I don't feel like I was really overworked on this.

Cheap: I'm sure that, if I shopped for a sale and used a coupon, I could get the store variety for less than I spent on the bread ingredients, but I think these compare pretty favorably to the retail price of a bag of croutons. After all, the bread itself is really less than $1 in ingredients, and I used maybe a tablespoon or two of butter. That's it.

Good: This is the reason to make your own. These really elevated a simple salad, and I was so glad to have that nice touch!

Cheap and Easy Spoonbread

A great use for frozen or canned corn is spoonbread, a kind of soft cornbread that includes whole kernel corn.

This quick recipe makes use of Jiffy cornbread mix. I like Jiffy mixes as the base for quick recipes; they are always cheap, and the ingredient list is generally pretty healthy and pretty much in line with what you would use if you made the recipe from scratch. This spoonbread requires:

Cheap and Easy Spoonbread
1 box Jiffy cornbread mix
1 egg
6 oz. milk
1 pint frozen or canned corn

Mix ingredients and spread in an 8x8 greased baking dish. Bake 25-30 minutes; longer baking creates a more bread-like product, while the lower time leaves it soft.

This is a great side dish for a meal, or a really good light meal. Eat the leftovers heated up in the mornings with butter and honey or maple syrup, or wait for lunch and add cheese (and maybe some diced chilies if you have them in the freezer or on the plant and feel like some heat).

The Analysis

Fast: One bowl, 4 ingredients, and about 32 minutes of prep including the baking time.

Cheap: Less than $1 for about 4 servings; even if you add ingredients to make a meal, it is still well within budget.

Good: Yummy and healthy, this is a great light meal or snack.

Homemade Pasta

If you have a good source of farm-raised, pastured eggs, one of the best ways of showing them off is by making homemade egg noodles.

We often think of homemade pasta as a time-intensive process that includes a lot of mess and a lot of rolling equipment to clean. In reality, most "peasant" cultures have developed quick ways of making pasta; it really should be considered a quick staple rather than an occasional treat.

To make homemade pasta you will need:

"Equal amounts" flour and eggs. That is, if you have three eggs, you need to use three cups of flour
Pinch of salt
Water as needed

Place the flour in a bowl and make a well in the center; crack the eggs into the well, and add the salt. Mix with water as needed to make a thick paste (the genesis of the word "pasta").

If you are pressed for time, you can then take this mixture by rounded spoonfuls and drop into a pot of boiling water; when the dumplings float, they are cooked. Or, if you have a little more time, you can roll the dough out into a sheet about a half an inch thick and cut into your desired shape with a pizza cutter or knife.

Cook the fresh pasta in salted boiling water until it floats; you will need to cook much less pasta than you normally do store-bought pasta, as this is denser and more filling. If you have cut your noodles thin enough, you can dry them by leaving them sitting out in on a cookie sheet.

The Analysis

Fast: It takes less time to make noodles than you think; remember, "peasant" food is nothing if not efficient to make.

Cheap: Most of your cost comes from the eggs; since my pastured eggs are nearly 30 cents apiece, a batch of pasta comes in at less than $1.75, and a batch generates at least four servings.

Good: Don't cover these up with heavy sauce; I like to have my homemade egg noodles with pasture butter and home grown sage. Yum.

Pumpkin "Gnocchi" with Rosemary and Leek Butter Sauce

3 c. flour
1 t. salt
3 eggs
Flesh of one small pie pumpkin, baked until soft and removed from skin
Water as needed

Combine all ingredients and add water only until you can handle and roll the dough. Roll into "snakes" on floured cutting board. Cut off small slices to make a small dumpling shape, and boil. (Mine were a bit big -- stick with penny or dime sized slices.) The pasta is ready when the dumplings float. You will have to do this in multiple batches unless you have a really huge, wide pan to boil in. The pasta stays nicely warm in a pan on the back of the stove.

While the pasta cooks, combine:

1/2 c. butter
1 leek, chopped
1 sprig of rosemary, finely chopped

Sauté the leek and rosemary in the butter.

When you have your pasta ready, dress it with the butter sauce, and serve with sea salt and fresh cracked pepper.

This is a great way to get some Vitamin A in your diet with the pumpkin, along with all the benefits of fresh, free-range eggs and healthy leeks. It is also a great vegetarian option, because I guarantee you won't want meat with this -- the dumpling "gnocchi" is quite meaty in texture.

The Analysis

Fast: Gnocchi takes some time to prepare, but it's an easy meal once you get the hang of it.

Cheap: Using some of your squash supply makes an already-cheap dish even more economical.

Good: If you are a pasta-lover like I am, you'll really enjoy this dish!

Tortellini and Four Cheese Sauce

Possibly my favorite Italian restaurant in the world is La Trattoria, located on Duval Street in Key West. They have a wonderful Tortellini alla Romana with tomatoes, peas, and smoked ham that I have to have at least once per trip "down island."

My own version is, well, not theirs, but it is enough to keep hopes alive for the next trip to Key West. And, if I do say so myself, it is pretty darn good.

1 c. whole milk
8 oz. Quattro Formaggio (four cheese) cheese blend
1 package pesto-filled tortellini
1 pint tomatoes
Scant cup ham (frozen leftover from previous holiday meal)
1 c. fresh peas (from the garden if possible)

Cook tomatoes, ham, and peas together until peas are tender. Meanwhile, boil pasta until just under al dente (it will cook more when combined).

Melt 8oz. of cheese in one cup whole milk until sauce consistency; you may have to add a tablespoon or two of flour to thicken to your desired thickness. Season with fresh cracked black pepper.

Combine all ingredients in sauté pan and cook until blended.

The Analysis:

Fast: The recipe took less than a half an hour to make.

Cheap: This recipe comes in at about $1.50 per serving for 4-5 servings, which compares very favorably to the restaurant meal. It can't bring you the island ambiance, however.

Good: Nothing is La Trattoria, but with some careful savings and yummy pasta dishes, I should be back "down island" before I know it!

Orecchiette Au Gratin with Farm-Fresh Corn, Leeks, and Sage

(When I developed this recipe, I was inspired by the long, involved food names used on so many of the cooking show. Feel free to call it "mac and cheese with corn" if you have a picky eater; otherwise, with the other title, you can charge $12 a plate for it!)

This is a great way to use some of the fresh corn from the farmer's market as well as the leeks that are starting to be ready at the same time. The introduction of the veggies means that you get to use less cheese, making it a lighter and less expensive dish. I did splurge on orecchiette pasta; literally meaning "little ears," these shapes are the perfect little bowls to hold the cheese sauce and corn while you eat. If you are seriously on a budget, try for a corkscrew or medium shell, which will do the same thing.

2-3 ears corn, cut from the cob
1-2 small leeks, cut and "split" so the little rings come apart
1 box orecchiette
1.5 cups whole milk
1 cup cheddar cheese
1 T flour
2 T sage
3/4 cup stuffing mix

Blanch your corn and cut off the cob while you are dicing leeks and boiling pasta to the al dente stage. Meanwhile, make your cheese sauce:

Melt cheese in milk over low heat. Add sage. 2 T is a lot, and I use that much because my family likes it, and because I have a surplus of dried sage from the garden. You may want to start with 1 T and work your way up if you are unsure. One note is that the sage gives "mac n cheese" dishes a very meaty flavor, so this is a good option if you are trying to coax a meat eater to join you in a vegetarian meal. Right before assembling the dish, add the flour for thickening and stir until thick and smooth.

Combine pasta, veggies, and cheese sauce in a casserole dish. Top with a crushed handful (about 3/4 cup) of stuffing mix. (You can use bread crumbs or cracker crumbs if you prefer, but I find many store brands of bread crumbs have HFCS. Make your own if you prefer, or use stuffing mix for a bit of an herby kick to the topping.)

Bake at 350 for about 25 minutes, until the cheese is bubbly.

The Analysis

Fast: You should be able to put this vegetarian meal on the table in under an hour, with much of it being cooking time.

Cheap: Garden and farmer's market veggies and a crumb topping mean you have to use less expensive cheese than you do for straight "mac n cheese." Cut costs further by not being seduced by the specialty pasta shapes, as I was!

Good: This has a gentle herb flavor and some crunch from the corn, leeks, and topping. It is a nice change from the heavier pasta dishes and makes a ton! (About 5 servings, I would estimate.)

Pumpkin Ravioli with Sage Butter

For New Year's weekend, I decided to go all out and make pumpkin ravioli with sage butter using as many locally-sourced ingredients as possible. It was a pretty time-consuming if yummy task, so I also devised a week-day version that comes together more quickly. Here's the description of the processes so you can compare:

Pumpkin Ravioli with Sage Butter: The Long Version

1. Prepare pumpkin puree. I had already done this step a few weeks ago when I decided it was finally time to do something with the pie pumpkins I had cellared from the fall farmer's market. Five pie pumpkins at 50 cents each gave me four pints of pumpkin puree plus a bunch of seeds to toast. I needed a pint for this recipe, so that is about 60 cents worth of pumpkin.

2. Prepare ricotta. This is where the "as local as possible" comes in. Rather than buying pre-made ricotta, I made my own from hormone-free milk. The milk was not local, unfortunately, but by making my own cheese I brought one of the processing steps home and eliminated some of the transportation and manufacturing costs. Ricotta from a half a gallon of milk came in under a dollar, and I used about half the batch, so maybe 50 cents of homemade ricotta.

3. In a food processor, mix pumpkin puree, ricotta, salt, fresh ground pepper, one clove of garlic, and a dash of nutmeg. The garlic came from my own garden via my cellar.

4. Make ravioli. Basically, these are the same noodles you saw in sage noodle soup, minus the sage. Roll out sheets of pasta dough, cut into large squares, and put a dollop of the filling in every other square. Moisten the edges with water and place a clean square of pasta dough on top and seal the edges. Although my flour and semolina were from the store, I used local eggs, and again, I removed a processing and transportation step from the equation, making these more local. Cutting and stuffing the ravioli takes some time, though! I estimate total cost for the pasta at under $1.

58

5. Drop ravioli one by one into boiling water and extract them when they float; it takes about 3-5 minutes depending on the thickness of your ravioli. I do these in waves and take the finished ravioli out with a slotted spoon and place them in a heat-safe bowl on the back of the stove while I cook subsequent batches.

6. Meanwhile, make sage butter. This is just butter (about half a cup) with a tablespoon of dried sage in it. I used fairly expensive but completely local butter, and the sage came from my garden. Total cost was probably $1 for this. Dress ravioli with sage butter, toss, and serve.

This version of the recipe was yummy, but boy did it take some time! So, I devised a short version that takes out the ravioli step, which is the most time consuming:

The Short Version

1. Make your pumpkin puree and your ricotta on another day. The puree will keep indefinitely in the freezer, and the ricotta will keep a week or two in the fridge.

2. Spray a baking dish with olive oil. Preheat oven to 350 degrees.

3. Cook lasagna noodles. You will probably need about 8-10 to use up your filling mixture.

4. On each noodle, spread a layer of filling. Sprinkle with additional ricotta. Roll up and place seam side down in baking dish.

5. Sprinkle each roll with sage and top with your favorite cheese. You might use mozzarella if you want a mild flavor or sharp cheddar if you want a contrast.

6. Bake about 20 minutes until cheese is melted.

Jennifer Patterson Lorenzetti

The Analysis

Fast: The long version took me a couple of hours to make, including time out for the use of some adult language when my pepper mill cap broke, sending peppercorns all over the kitchen. Nonetheless, I think I now know why ravioli is a special-occasion dish.

Cheap: By relying on my own herbs and pumpkin from the farmer's market, I kept costs way down. Making my own ricotta also saved money. Total cost for the long version was just over $3.

Good: The long version with homemade ingredients is far superior to any other version, but it does take some time. The short version does a nice job of preserving the pumpkin flavor while being a bit easier to put together.

Pesto-dressed Pasta with Garden Veggies and Mizithra Cheese

Garden veggies make for great frugal opportunities to try artisanal cheeses and meats that are normally so expensive if they are the feature of a dish. This is a technique called "stretching." Your grandmother or great-grandmother did this during WWII or the Depression, and it is how you take a pound of hamburger, add an egg (frequently from at-home laying hens in the era, even in suburban homes) and some oats or crackers or bread, and get a meatloaf that feeds a family of 6-8.

Here, I am using my garden veggies to stretch some yummy Greek Mizithra cheese, which is typically $10 or more per pound, way more expensive than I would typically be willing to pay for cheese. However, let's see how I stretched it:

1 box pasta
2 oz. Mizithra cheese
1/2 pint pesto (frozen from garden; free – see recipe next page)
6-8 medium tomatoes (garden; free)
2 small leeks (garden; free)
2 cloves garlic (garden; free)
1 mild chili (garden; free)
sea salt and cracked black pepper

Cook pasta until al dente. Coat with basil pesto, add salt to taste, and set aside.

Meanwhile, cut tomatoes into chunks and sauté with leeks, garlic, and the chopped, de-seeded chili. When the tomatoes have cooked down, but are not mush (about 10 minutes), strain the juice off and top the pasta. Add about 2 oz. of Mizithra cheese and serve.

Makes 4 large servings. It refrigerates and reheats well, so if you have a small family or live alone, you can easily make dinner and then package up the leftovers for lunch at the office or dinner the next day.

The Analysis

Fast: I made this twice over a single weekend, so enamored of it were we. It takes about 30 minutes total of active cooking.

Cheap: Other than the base cost of growing a garden, the veggies are "free," so the pasta and cheese are the only costs. This meal easily comes in under $0.75 per serving.

Good: Try this with your favorite gourmet cheese. A strongly-flavored cheese like Mizithra doesn't require a lot to pack a punch, so you will be enjoying this yummy meal all the way to the bank!

Roasted Blue Potato Salad

I'm not usually a fan of potato salad, but I have recently developed a recipe I really like, based on tips from several recipes I consulted. This is a great way to show off those garden potatoes you have down cellar, and the best thing is that it can be served hot, room temp, or cold, which makes it a great recipe for taking to those get-togethers where you aren't sure if you will have oven access when you get there. (Note: The dressing does contain mayo, so I'm not telling you to leave this sitting out all day. Decide if you will be able to heat the potatoes and dress it onsite, or if you will be taking a chilled dish, and plan accordingly.)

8-12 blue potatoes (you can sub in some Yukon Golds or another "normal" color if you like), diced
2 medium leeks, diced
1 sprig rosemary, chopped
1 pat pasture butter

Preheat oven to 350. Mix all ingredients and bake until potatoes are soft, stirring occasionally.

In the meantime, mix the dressing:
1/2 cup organic mayo
1/2 cup lime juice
1 T mustard -- dijon or plain

When potatoes are ready, dress with the dressing. Serve.

The Analysis

Fast: This recipe takes about 45 minutes, most of which is baking time.

Cheap: I depend on cellared potatoes, still-growing leeks, and rosemary from the front window to make it practically free.

Good: It reheats well and is great for a hot lunch for me and a cold snack for Mr. FC&G. Yum!

Basil Pesto

If I had to pick only two things to grow in my garden, they would be tomatoes and basil. Tomatoes because nothing tastes like a home grown tomato, and basil because it functions almost as a cash crop for me.

Nothing could be easier than growing basil. Packets of seeds of "Genovese" or "common" basil, the kind that is perfect for pesto and sauces, are readily available at the hardware and grocery store every spring for around $1.50. (Yes, they are hybrids; if you want an all-heirloom garden, you will pay up. But I promise, Genovese or common basil is the kind you want for pesto -- meaty, large leaves, strong aroma, dark green color.) Start your seeds about 6 weeks before your last frost date; I usually dump about a quarter of a pack of seeds into each of four small pots and treat the resulting seedlings as four plants. Wait until your ground is warm and no threat of frost remains, and plant them in a sunny spot.

You will wait forever to see a plant of any size, but when it starts to take off, prune the plant regularly at the leaf junctions, encouraging two more branches to sprout where you cut. Pretty soon, you will have a basil plant of mammoth proportions.

I think the best way to preserve the bounty is by making pesto. Pesto (coming from the Italian root for "paste," the same as pasta) is a sauce of any leafy green mixed with olive oil, salt, and frequently cheese and or nuts. I use the term "pesto" to refer to basil and oil, to which I add salt when I cook. I may or may not want to add cheese or other inputs, so I freeze it pretty plain.

In the store, small jars (3 oz.) of basil pesto are typically $3.39 (the most common price I saw when I looked at a few brands). If you assume that each ounce requires 38 cents worth of non-basil inputs (like oil and salt), making your own basil pesto will save you 75 cents per ounce. This can get into some serious savings quickly. One year, I froze 14 half pint containers of pesto (a half pint will cover a box of pasta, which is my most typical usage). That means 112 ounces, or $84 in savings over buying a comparable amount in the store. As you can see, most years the basil pesto alone will pay for a significant part of the garden seeds and plants (which typically run me around $250 a year).

To make pesto, wash your basil leaves and puree in a food processor with olive oil until you have a consistency somewhere between a sauce and a paste. Put in a container and freeze.

You can use this to dress pasta, giving you a quick meal that also has a fair amount of leafy green veg in it. Or, use it as a compliment to dipping oil for bread, or as a dressing between veg and bread on bruschetta. When you use it, you can add salt, cheese, or nuts to your liking. In the winter, I love to make a batch of pasta with basil pesto, sea salt, sun dried tomatoes, and a grating of Parmesan as a quick, healthy meal.

The Analysis

Fast: Processing basil to be frozen takes a little time, but not as much time as, say, freezing strawberries or canning tomatoes.

Cheap: See above. Every 8 oz. container of pesto you freeze now saves you $6 over buying the cute little jars in the store.

Good: Here's the kicker: nothing tastes as good basil pesto frozen the day it was picked, so the expensive little jars don't even taste as good!

Cheesy Potato Soup

Including a vegetarian meal at least once a week is a quick way to reduce your food bills while upping your consumption of veggies. This soup is hearty, satisfying, and will have you warmed up in no time after a day of shoveling snow.

2 T butter (Pasture butter if you can find it.)
1 c diced onions (From the root cellar if you have thought ahead.)
2 1/2 c diced potatoes, unpeeled (From the root cellar; I like the yellow potatoes if you are making a purchase.)
3 c chicken broth (Organic free range is nice; making your own is nicer)
1 c heavy cream (Organic, again)
2 c shredded cheddar cheese (Hormone free, if possible)
1 T dill weed (Dried from the summer makes it free.)
1/8 t ground cayenne pepper (Ditto on dried from summer.)
A few grinds of salt and pepper

In a large saucepan, sauté onions in the butter until they are translucent. Stir in potatoes and broth and let cook until potatoes are softened.

When potatoes are softened to your liking, add cream, spices, and cheese. Cook until cheese is melted. If you are using dill you dried yourself, you will see it "bloom" open, adding a lovely green speckle against the pale yellow of the soup.

Makes 4 servings. Maybe 3 if you have been shoveling snow.

The Analysis

Fast: This takes at most 45 minutes to prep and cook. Not as fast as a can of soup, but darn quick in the homemade soup world.

Cheap: This recipe, like many others, is scalable by budget. Using organic free range broth and organic cream will drive up the price a bit, but these are choices I make because I am not happy with how CAFO animals are treated, and the organic options are at least some better. On the other hand, relying on home-dried spices and cellared root vegetables will keep the price low.

Good: Much heartier and healthier than the glop from a can.

Sage Noodle Soup

Here's a great, hearty soup that relies almost entirely on homemade and homegrown ingredients.

Sage Noodles:
1 cup regular flour
1 cup semolina flour
2 eggs (local farm-raised with lovely orange yolks)
1 t. salt
sage to taste (I used about 1 T of the dried from the summer)
water to make thick paste

Turn out on floured board and knead in the flour until no longer sticky. Roll with rolling pin until about 1/2 inch thick and cut into whatever size you like (although I like about an inch by an inch and a half for soup). Cook by boiling until they float in the rapidly boiling water. (I cook mine separately so the leftovers don't create bloated noodles by leaving them in the soup. This also keeps the starch that boils off the noodles out of the soup, so you have a clear soup.)

Soup:
While this is going on, bring the following to a boil and then reduce to a simmer:

1 qt. chicken stock
1 onion, diced
1 pint frozen corn
1 T. sage
1 T. marjoram
Optional--a few diced green chilies, for heat
salt and pepper

When corn is cooked and onions are translucent, place some of the noodles in each serving bowl and top with soup. Repeat as needed. (I usually double this recipe so I have leftovers. If you do, you only need to double the soup and not necessarily the noodles.)

The Analysis

Fast: I made this batch of soup in under an hour, which is a long prep time for me but very enjoyable on a cold Sunday afternoon. You can make the soup part in the crock pot if you prefer, which means that part can cook while you are at work.

Cheap: By having an inexpensive local source of eggs and a lot of herbs and peppers at my disposal, this was not an expensive recipe. Making your own chicken stock in the future is a good next step to frugal soup.

Good: The sage noodles really boost this soup from ordinary to special. I am really working on natural healing endeavors right now, and there is a reason that chicken soup is called "Jewish Penicillin." The onions, peppers, sage, and marjoram all have properties that will help out if you have a cold.

Butternut Squash Soup

We have had a couple of really good years for butternut squash. If I grow a half a row of these easy-to-store veggies, I usually get ten pounds or more of fruit to store downstairs, which is plenty to get us through the winter. Plus, I love that the seeds are so easy to extract and save; this past year, I grew all of our butternut squash from saved seeds, which meant that the entire harvest was free!

Of course, that means we have to eat the squash, and my new favorite recipe is butternut squash soup. It is pretty easy for this recipe to be entirely local even in winter, since it is primarily made of storage veggies, stock, and herbs. Or, if you are like me, you can do a combo of store-bought and homegrown veggies.

The base soup is very mild, so you can alter the herbs to your own taste. I tried to pick some flavors that would give it a warm kick, which seemed just right in winter.

1 T. butter
1 small/medium onion, diced
1 clove garlic, diced
1 medium carrot, diced
4 small Yukon Gold potatoes, diced
1 medium or 2 small butternut squash, peeled, seeded, and cubed
1 quart stock (I used homemade chicken stock)
salt and fresh ground pepper to taste
marjoram (about 1 T. dried leaves, crushed to 1 t.)
curry powder, about 1/2 to 1 t., to taste

Melt butter in large stock pot and cook onions and garlic until wilted and clear. Add remaining vegetables and stock, and cook until veggies are soft, about 30-40 minutes. Add herbs and spices and cook about 5 minutes more. Puree until smooth with immersion blender.

Makes 2 large servings.

The Analysis

Fast: This soup takes about an hour of active cooking and prep, what with all of the chopping and blending, but it is totally worth it.

Cheap: If you still have a cellar full of veggies and stock, you might be able to make this totally from your stores. Otherwise, feel free to shop for the veggies you need. I bought the carrots, potatoes, and onions.

Good: We had no leftovers from this batch, so that tells you how much we enjoyed it. It would be easy to make this recipe entirely vegetarian if you use vegetable stock, or vegan if you also omit the butter (use a smidge of olive oil to cook your onions).

Whipped Butternut Squash

If you're a gardener, you know what I'm talking about here: It's January, there's snow up to your knees (if you live in the north), and the seed catalogs arrive. And before you know it, you're ordering things you've never grown and that you don't know how to prepare.

"I'll figure that out when it ripens," you think. "But that looks darn fun to grow!"

And that's how I ended up growing butternut squash, creating a bit of a panic attack when about a dozen of the lovely little guys started ripening this week, and I had no idea what to do with them.

Enter whipped butternut squash, perhaps one of my new favorite side dishes. It is kind of a cross between mashed potatoes and sweet potatoes in flavor, for those who haven't had it

This dish delivers a punch of vitamin A that makes growing the squash worthwhile. Best of all, winter squash cellars well, so I can cure a crop of these babies and put them downstairs, awaiting the day this winter that I need a yummy side dish while I read the seed catalogs.

1. Cut 2 butternut squash in half and remove seeds for next year's crop. Place cut side down in baking dishes filled with about an inch of water. Bake at 350 until soft, about 35 minutes for the squash I had.
2. Scoop out the flesh into a bowl. Add about a quarter cup of scalded milk and a quarter cup of brown sugar. Whip with your mixer until creamy.
3. Top with a mixture of butter and brown sugar to taste. As this topping sinks in, it gets even yummier, so leftovers are wonderful!

The Analysis

Fast: Although about 45-50 minutes elapsed during prep, most was baking the squash. And luckily, Mr. FC&G was around to do the hard work of cutting a winter squash.

Cheap: If you grow your own squash, this recipe requires only the milk, butter, and brown sugar to taste.

Good: I really like this recipe, and I would also suggest it for those who like mashed potatoes or sweet potatoes but need or want to get another veggie in their diet!

Red, White, and Blue Potatoes

I am not the type to make specific foods colored for certain holidays (those red, white, and blue Jell-O parfaits from the 1970s make me cringe), but this Fourth of July I made a dish that is a riff on holiday colors to illustrate two points about sustainable living. First, the recipe:

6 red skin potatoes, sliced thin
3 blue potatoes, sliced thin
2 ears corn, cut from cob
1 onion, diced
1-2 cloves garlic, crushed
1 cup shredded parmesan
1 handful fresh thyme
A few grinds black pepper and sea salt

Preheat oven to 350. Boil water and throw in ears of corn to blanch so you can more easily cut them off the cob. This is not a true food preservation blanching -- you just want a little cooking to soften things up.

While the corn is blanching, cut your red skin potatoes and form in a layer in a small baking dish (a couple of spritzes of olive oil on the bottom will keep things from sticking). Then, in a bowl, cut the corn off the cob, and combine with onion, garlic, 3/4 cup of parmesan, chopped thyme, and salt and pepper. Mix well and put on top of the potato layer. Add another layer of red skin and blue potato slices and the remaining cheese. Bake for 45 minutes or until cheese is melted and potatoes are soft. I covered mine with foil for about 25 minutes and then took the foil off -- save it to cover the dish in the fridge if you have leftovers.

Lesson One
Our first lesson is that sustainable living is about making do with what you have, not starting with what you want and procuring the inputs. That is, I had red skin potatoes and corn from the farmer's market, onions in the pantry, and blue potatoes and thyme in the

garden. I figured out how to cook them all to be sure they would not go to waste.

However, I don't really want you going out and trying to buy all of these ingredients (unless they are all at your local farmer's market). Sustainability isn't about opting not to make a dish because you need a quarter teaspoon of lemon zest (and I have been guilty of the equivalent of going out and buying a bag of lemons and a zester to make this happen, just as everyone does from time to time). Sustainability is about using your current bounty. I could have made this dish equally well with any hearty veggies I could bake and pretty much any cheese or herbs. For example, try:

- Zucchini
- Leeks
- Paste tomatoes
- Oregano
- Basil
- Cilantro
- Cheddar
- Mozzarella

I'm sure this is just a partial list. For example, even though I love the corn in this iteration, I don't really need it: zucchini and onion bakes up just as well with dried sage and cheddar.

Lesson Two
Get outside the traditional supermarket, and you will find many variations on standard veggies that will improve your diet. Blue potatoes, which I grow because they are pretty and they are hard to find elsewhere, have some of the same phytochemicals that make blueberries blue. These phytochemicals may be necessary for optimum health, but it is tough to find a blue food beyond berries and eggplant.

So, if you have a family member who likes only potatoes, you can improve their intake of a variety of phytochemicals by including blue, red skin, yellow, and fingerling potatoes in addition to plain brown bakers. Carrots come in orange, yellow, white, and red (their original color, some say). Tomatoes come in yellow, red, green, and deep purple, among other colors. This is not an argument to limit one's veggie consumption but rather to broaden it by exploring a well-loved category. And hey, once you talk your fussy potato-lover into a blue potato, he may be willing to try a blueberry.

The Analysis

Fast: This dish takes about 20 minutes of prep (a little more if you are out sticking your hands in the potato hills, like I was) and about 45 minutes to bake.

Cheap: This depends greatly on how much you have to buy. I'd say I spent about $3 since I had to buy a few farmer's market potatoes and ears of corn, an onion, and some cheese. Later in the season, the only thing I'll be buying is the cheese.

Good: I think this makes a great grill-out side dish; if you are mostly-vegetarian like me, this is a hearty main dish.

Sautéed Root Veggies

New potatoes
New carrots
Any other dense veggies you may have pulled from the garden; the
other night, we added the first zucchini and the last of the peas

Garden garlic -- 2 cloves
Garden dill
2 T. butter
Salt and Pepper

Melt butter in a sauté pan and add chopped garlic. Add diced veggies
in order of how long you want them to cook; for the above photo, I
chopped potatoes first, then carrots. Salt and pepper liberally, then
add chopped fresh dill. Sauté until desired tenderness.

The Analysis

Fast: This takes about 20-25 minutes to cook, and you can pretty
much chop while you cook if you do your veggies in the order of
density.

Cheap: Since we had potatoes, carrots, garlic, and dill all in the
garden or pantry, I only paid for butter and seasonings. That's my
kind of dish!

Good: The garlic and dill really made the dish for us. It turned this
from your generic mixed veggies or hash browns into something
really special.

Zucchini Pie

I love zucchini more than I ever would have thought possible when I was a kid. (For that matter, I don't think I knew what zucchini were as a kid.) This recipe is another favorite around our house, and we make this dish at least once a week when the zucchini are in season. It is a great way to introduce a vegetarian dish into your diet if you don't normally go veggie, because the texture of the zucchini is very hearty and toothsome.

FC&G Zucchini Pie

1 double pie crust
1 medium zucchini, sliced
1 medium onion (or equivalent), sliced
1 head garlic, chopped
1 handful fresh thyme, chopped
1.5 cups cheddar or cheddar blend cheese
1/2 cup yellow mustard

Mix veggies in a bowl to combine the zucchini and onion with the thyme and garlic. Let sit while you make the pie crust.

In a deep dish pie pan, lay bottom crust and coat with the yellow mustard. Layer the veggies in, and top with the cheese. (You can alternate cheese and veggie if you have a lot of veggies to use up.) Top with pie crust.

Bake in 350 degree oven until crust is done and veggies tender, about 40 minutes.

The Analysis

Fast: Mr. FC&G and I work together on this; he makes his famous flaky pie crust, and I chop veggies. Then it is just sit and wait until the pie is done.

Cheap: With all of the veggies coming from the garden, the only costs associated with this dish are the cheese and the flour and lard needed for the crust. This dish regularly comes in at around $5 and provides about 4-5 servings.

Good: This is a great way to use your summer zucchini and get a lot of healthy squash and root veggies in your diet. It reheats very well; I think it's even better the next day. To really maximize your oven time, make a batch of zucchini bread to bake alongside the pie.

Mr. FC&G's Flaky Pie Crust

(Editor's Note: I have begged Mr. FC&G for a while to share his flaky pie crust recipe with the blogosphere. Being an engineer, this resulted in his conducting many tests (yum!) and getting the recipe perfect for you before he would share it. One morning, I woke up to discover him authoring a blog post. This is almost as good as the days I wake up to a mug of hot coffee that he has prepared!)

One of the many advantages of being Mr. FC&G is that I get to eat my share of the vegetables that come in from the garden. This has been a good year for zucchini so we have been enjoying lots of one of my favorite recipes, zucchini pie. Something I figured out about zucchini pies is that I can have them more often if I help out by making the crusts.

Our recipe is adapted from the one in *Betty Crocker's Picture Cook Book*. We have a facsimile edition of the 1950 original. Zucchini pie wants a thick crust, so I have scaled up the ingredient quantities by 150 percent. Also, we switched to using lard instead of shortening about a year ago.

When I first started using lard, the dough became too fragile to roll out and transfer to the pie pan. Naturally the first thing to try was putting in more lard, but that just made the problem worse. It was taking three or four tries to get a salvageable crust (and I'm not too proud to piece a broken one together in the pan). It turns out the way to go was to use less lard. This made sense once I thought about it. It must be the lard or shortening that turns a glue recipe into a dough recipe.

We buy our lard at a local farmer's market. The tub we have now came from Morning Sun Farm in West Alexandria, Ohio, and the lard just melts in your hand, even coming straight from the refrigerator. That seems like a good thing to me (someone will have to comment if that's not what it's supposed to do). During the winter we can also run up to Landes Meats in Englewood, Ohio.

This makes enough dough for a two-crust pie, using an eight or nine inch pan.

3 cups flour (or 2-1/2 cups flour plus ½ cup whole-wheat flour)
1-1/2 tsp. salt
2/3 cup rendered lard (or 1 cup shortening)
6 tbsp. water (to start with)
Optional for dessert pies: 1 cup sugar

1. Mix the dry ingredients in a large bowl.
2. Cut in the lard.
3. Add the water a little at a time. Mix it in lightly until all the flour is moist.
4. Form the dough in to a ball using your hands.
5. Take about 2/3 of the dough and roll it out to form a thick bottom crust.
6. Transfer to pie pan, then trim.
7. Ball up remaining dough and roll it out to form the top crust.

I use unbleached flour because that's the FC&G way. Recently I came up a little short of flour and had to throw in a half a cup of whole-wheat flour. The crust turned out really yummy, so I have kept on doing that for zucchini pie. (I doubt this would be so good in a dessert pie).

I used to just mash the lard together with the dry ingredients using my fingers. Recently I re-read the Betty Crocker recipe and realized they have some tricks for making the crust tender and flaky. Betty recommends cutting in half the shortening with a pastry blender to make a fine mixture that looks like meal. This makes the crust tender. Then she says to cut in the rest of the shortening coarsely so that you get particles the size of "giant peas". This is supposed to make the pastry flaky. I don't own a pastry blender, so I've been using a fork for this. I also haven't been getting the giant-peas thing working, so maybe I should get the pastry blender after all. From the pictures it looks like a pastry blender is one of those "D" shaped tools where the handle is the straight side, and the curved side is formed from loops of wire.

Measuring out the water for this recipe is probably a waste of time. I always seem to wind up adding a little more or less to get the consistency I want. Mix the water in a little at a time with a fork.

Rolling out the dough is the messy part of the process. I lay down a couple sheets of wax paper and spread some flour on them. Next take about 2/3 of the dough and mash it out in to a thick patty on the wax paper. Dust the top with flour, then turn the patty over and dust it with flour again. Use a rolling pin to roll the dough out in to a sheet a little larger than the pie pan. I like a thick crust for zucchini pie, so I roll it out just a little thicker than I might for a dessert pie.

To transfer the pastry to the pie pan I like the trick of rolling it up loosely on the rolling pin, then unrolling it over the pan.

Trim the extra dough off. Use scrap pieces to repair any rips in the pastry. Throw the left over scraps back in the bowl and ball them up with the dough for the top crust.

Make the top crust the same way.

Once the pie is assembled, cutting the vent holes is an important step. If you are making the pie for company then you might want to use something traditional like lots of perfectly cut slits. Otherwise, the vent is a perfect opportunity to tease your loved ones by cutting in a picture based on an inside joke. I have a design that makes sense to Jennifer that would take way too much effort to explain to anyone else!

There is also a sweet trick for dessert pies that someone showed me long ago. Along with the other dry ingredients; mix in one cup of sugar.

The Analysis (by Jennifer)

Fast: I hate making pie crusts, so the only way pie is going to happen around here is if Mr. FC&G makes the crust while I make the filling.

Cheap: Flour, lard, and salt. Not that expensive.

Good: Flakey and yummy, Mr. FC&G's crusts are the highlight of any pie. Combine with homegrown zucchini or farmers' market berries, and you have a real sustainable treat!

Thai Basil Salmon and Swiss Chard

I'm not really a huge fan of Asian-inspired flavors in my cooking, preferring instead to use Mediterranean and Cuban influences. However, I am a big fan of Thai basil, and I grew a beautiful huge plant in the herb garden in 2010, enough for fresh Thai basil all summer as well as a stock of dried and frozen. The last of the frozen basil in oil was in the freezer, so it was time to experiment with a way of using it.

This recipe takes inspiration from my mojito salmon. Prices of wild-caught Alaskan salmon have really gone up; I think this package came in around $8 for two pieces. I still think it is a worthwhile centerpiece to the meal, especially since everything else came from the spice cabinet or the garden.

1 package wild-caught Alaskan Salmon (2 fillets)
1/2 pint Thai basil chopped and frozen in oil (or a comparable amount of fresh, plus some olive oil for the pan)
curry powder
smoked sea salt
baby Swiss chard (from the sunroom)

Place the salmon fillets in a pan and sprinkle with curry powder and smoked sea salt. Plop the frozen Thai basil in. If you are using fresh basil, you will want to put a dollop of oil in the pan and then place the chopped basil on top of the seasoned fish.

Bake at 350 until done, about 30 minutes for the fillets I used. Reach in the oven once in a while and stir the Thai basil around and make sure it is coated with oil and sitting nicely on top of the fish. This keeps the basil hydrated and makes it wilt rather than dry out and get crispy and burnt. When done, place each fillet on top of chopped baby Swiss chard, being sure to dress both fish and chard with the now-baked Thai basil, and serve.

The Analysis

Fast: I love baked fish dishes because you just season the fish and stick it in the oven. Fish goes so well over greens that we often omit the starch for these meals.

Cheap: Fish prices are on the rise, but I basically got one large serving and a couple of small ones out of this package of salmon, which was around $8.

Good: To me, this was just the right hint of curry and Thai basil to suggest Asian flavors but not overwhelm. If you love the Asian flavor profiles, you can go all-out with more curry and some roasted chilies.

Berries and Cream Smoothies

A traditional smoothie is made with yogurt, ice cubes, and unsugared berries. It is very virtuous. But I don't like yogurt, and I have a freezer full of strawberries (preserved with sugar) each year that need to start vacating to make room for this year's crop. So I devised this quick and easy smoothie:

1 quart berries, thawed (sugared if you prefer or have preserved them that way)
1/2 cup heavy whipping cream (from hormone-free milk and pasteurized but not ultrapasteurized)

Place in blender and blend. Makes 2.5 large servings (the half serving is pictured above!)

The Analysis:

Fast: If you remember to thaw your berries, this takes only a few seconds in the blender to make a couple of days' worth of smoothie for one person, or an excellent huge serving of berries for each of two people.

Cheap: The whipping cream was $2.49 for a pint, so $0.62 for a half cup. That means the entire recipe comes in at less than $1.00, figure by guess-timating the amount of sugar and you-pick berries I added. That means you can have a good snack or a reasonable meal substitute for less than $0.50.

Good: This is an easy way to get a lot of fruit, some protein from the dairy, and enough fat to aid your body's absorption of the vitamins. Plus, more freezer space for this year's berries!

Homemade Yogurt

I tend to think of making dairy products as something of an advanced sustainability skill. I have made cheese, and it requires a fair amount of thought (and a good source of milk that has not been overly pasteurized, which is harder to obtain than you might think). I have made sour cream, and it is fairly easy, but I have typically wound up with enough sour cream to stock a small Mexican restaurant.

Homemade yogurt, however, is a different story, and it a superstar in both the budget and the end product.

It couldn't be easier. Take your milk (I use a half gallon, but the recipe is totally scalable to the amount you need; there is no reason why you couldn't make anything from a pint to a gallon) and scald it, which means bringing it to a temperature of 180 to 190. I have a dairy thermometer to measure this, but you could use a candy thermometer in a pinch.

Then, let the milk cool to between 110 and 120 degrees. Stir in a couple of tablespoons of yogurt; I buy a container of organic vanilla yogurt to get my batch started, but future batches can be made from the last couple of spoons of the existing batch. Put it in a covered container (I use a half gallon Mason jar), wrap with a towel, and let sit where it will drop no lower than 95 degrees. This may take some doing in the winter, but in summer I just tote it outside or into the sun room and sit it on a high plant shelf.

Don't disturb it; you are waiting for the good bacteria to grow to the point that they culture the entire batch, at which point it will be thick. This takes about 4-5 hours. Refrigerate.

Mr. FC&G notes that he likes this yogurt better than store-bought varieties. I'm not much of a yogurt-eater, but I like this a lot. It is milder than the store varieties. And it is a yummy vehicle for some blackberry preserves.

(Note: If you are packing a lunch, you could take a half pint Mason jar, add yogurt and preserves, and have your own little fruit and yogurt snack with very much the look and feel of a conventional yogurt container.)

The Analysis

Fast: I'd say a batch takes about 20 minutes of active scalding and cooling, plus the 4-5 hours of letting it sit.

Cheap: You will make 64 ounces of yogurt for the price of a half-gallon of milk, plus a small container of organic yogurt as starter if needed. This is far less than buying the finished yogurt.

Good: Light, mild, and creamy, this may be my new favorite homemade food.

Homemade Sour Cream

Remember all that money we are saving on veggies by growing our own? Well, it is time to spend a little, because one of the things that most sustainable-living sources don't point out is that finding high-quality, sustainably-produced dairy products is sometimes difficult, and when you find them, you will be paying up for them.

Why am I not just grabbing a gallon of whatever milk is on sale?

- Hormones: I want a milk that is from cows not treated with hormones to make them produce more milk. Although the government notes that the hormone is not detectable in the final milk or cheese, I don't believe our bodies can't detect it. And frankly, I feel "puffier" when I eat dairy that contains the hormones. That's subjective, of course, but I still would prefer to avoid the hormone.

- Grass-fed: Here's the thing -- cows are ruminants, which means that they have stomachs (two each, actually) that are designed to digest grasses. However, corn and grain cause them no end of problems. The final milk product from a grass-fed cow has a higher level of CLA, which is thought to ward off cancer and other problems. And, allowing cows to live like cows is inherently kinder to them.

- Cream line: I just uncovered evidence that homogenized milk, in which the fat globules are broken up to mix in the cream and save you the terrible task of actually shaking the milk before you pour it, might contribute to higher levels of cholesterol in the body. It seems the larger fat globules in non-homogenized milk actually are handled by your body better.

OK, so I want a hormone-free product from grass-fed cows who ate pesticide- and herbicide-free grass and gave milk that the bottler did not homogenize. I don't want much, do I? When I find this product, I want to make as many of my dairy products as possible from it to boost the health benefits to us and get the most bang for my buck.

To make sour cream, then, I poured a half gallon of milk into a bowl and let it sit overnight in the refrigerator, then skimmed the cream. I got nearly a quart of cream/thicker milk to which I added just a bit of half and half to make a whole quart. I then heated the cream to 86 degrees and stirred in the sour cream starter culture and let the whole thing sit with a towel wrapped around it for 12 hours.

Bingo! Sour cream. I think the non-homogenized cream really made it a lot thicker, and homemade sour cream is generally milder in flavor than store-bought.

The Analysis

Fast: Actual hands-on time was fairly minimal, although this is a two-day project once you count letting the cream rise and then letting the sour cream sit and thicken.

Cheap: Oh, heck no. My oh-so-healthy milk was $3.50 a half gallon in 2011, plus $1.50 bottle deposit. The sour cream culture will set you back another $1.20 a packet plus shipping. With dairy, you either go healthy or cheap, but there is very little middle ground. If this simply puts this project out of reach for you financially, consider upgrading to organic sour cream, which by definition will not have hormones or exposure to certain pesticides and herbicides.

Good: It is very hard to find sour cream that meets all the conditions set out above for milk, so making it is my only option. The end product is really much better-tasting, I think, and it is worth the extra money.

Ham and Other Stock

One of the most traditional ways to stretch the number of meals you get out of your meat purchases is to make stock from the bones and trimmings. If you are a meat-eater, this is a great, low-cost way to get maximum value from your meat investment. If you are mostly vegetarian, then it is a good way to get a little animal protein in your diet without actually having a meat-heavy meal.

For a batch of ham stock, I took the bone and the tough "butt" of the ham from our Easter dinner. I put it in a large stew pot, covered it with water, and simmered for an hour with a diced onion, a couple of bay leaves, and some cracked black pepper.

When the stock is done, it can be frozen in quart freezer containers or pressure canned in quart jars. I prefer the pressure canning because the final product doesn't take up valuable freezer real estate.

I believe the ham took less time to make a decent stock because it is already seasoned and cured, so the flavor develops more quickly.. Beef and chicken take more like 3-4 hours, so plan ahead to do this on a weekend or a day or evening when you want to be in the kitchen to smell the great smells. Depending on the meat you use, you may have to skim fat off the stock before you freeze it.

I keep a "stock bucket" in the freezer for meat trimmings, bones, and veggie trimmings like onion stalks; when it is full and I have time, I make and can another batch of stock.

The Analysis

Fast: Although this took an hour, there was nearly no prep time, so I just needed to find a time I was near the kitchen doing something else so I could keep an eye on the stock pot.

Cheap: For the price of an onion and some spices, I took a chunk of ham that would have been wasted and made the basis of a future meal. For reference, a quart of organic broth at the store is typically at least $2.50, so you can count on saving at least $2 per quart you can, once you take into account any inputs you purchased.

Good: The smell alone is worth the time investment!

Mojito Salmon

I loved mojitos before they were popular. This combination of lime, mint, cane sugar, and rum in a sparkling club soda base is infinitely refreshing on a hot summer day. What you may not know is that the basic set of mojito flavor -- lime, mint, sugar -- work well in a lot of culinary applications.

One of my favorite recipes is Mojito Salmon. You will need:

1 package wild caught salmon (2 large pieces)
1 handful mojito mint* (I grow this in the garden)
Juice of 3-4 limes, or a comparable amount of bottled
Sea Salt
Fresh Ground pepper
Olive Oil
(You can add a bit of cane sugar if you prefer a sweeter marinade.)

Chop and crush the mint, and place on top of the thawed salmon. Drizzle with olive oil and lime juice, then sprinkle with salt and pepper. Put in the fridge for a couple of hours so the flavors blend.

Cook in a 350 oven until salmon is done, about 20-30 minutes according to the thickness of your pieces and how many you have in the pan.

To serve, cook some yellow rice and top the rice with shredded garden greens and fresh garden peas. Place the cooked salmon on top. The heat from the salmon and rice will wilt the greens and warm the peas without really cooking them, so they maintain a crunch.

*I grow genuine mojito mint. You can make any mojito drink or dish with any available mint, but this mint has a deeper flavor and a bit less sweetness to it. If you grow traditional spearmint, start all of your mojito projects with less cane sugar and adjust to your own taste. I also freeze mojito mint in oil the same way I do cilantro, and then I just thaw the mint and oil at the same time I do the salmon, then combine the whole mess along with the other ingredients to marinate.

The Analysis

Fast: I can bang out this dinner in about 45 minutes, with much of that being baking time. I am not counting the marinating time, because I'm really doing nothing at that point.

Cheap: Depending on how many of the ingredients you need to buy versus how many you can grow, this dish probably comes in at $10.00, which is usually my upper limit for "nice dinner at home." This recipe served with the rice and spring garden veggies gives us two dinners and two small lunches.

Good: Healthy, summery, and just a little bit Cuban in influence. Mix up some actual mojitos to go alongside, and you are all set.

Salmon Patties

This recipe is courtesy of Mom FC&G: Salmon Patties

1 can or pouch salmon (6-7 oz.) -- look for wild caught domestic if you can
1/2 sleeve of saltine crackers, crushed
1 egg
1 t. Worcestershire sauce
1/2 t. mustard powder (I often up this to 1 t.)

"Sort" the salmon to remove any skin or bones that have been included in the package. (You could use the flaked leftovers from fillets you grilled, as well.) Mix with the rest of the ingredients and form into about 4 patties. Fry in olive oil until golden brown on each side, about 3-5 minutes per side.

Serve with sautéed garden veggies -- use whatever is ready in your garden.

The Analysis

Fast: These patties are ready in a jiff! Experiment with the salmon you use; I have unfortunately found a trade-off to be made between brands that are "clean" (don't include a lot of bones and skin) and brands that are domestic, wild caught product.

Cheap: As a meat-stretcher recipe, this probably comes in at under $3. If you have some garden veggies to flesh things out, you will probably get 3-4 servings of food for under $4 total.

Good: This has always been one of my favorite recipes, so of course I love it and wanted to share it with you.

Pork Sausage

There is a truism that there are two things you should never watch being made: laws and sausage. So I try to avoid watching CSPAN as much as possible; that's easy. However, sausage is one of the few meats I actually like, and believe me, I like ground, spiced meat from any culture, in almost any flavor profile you can name. I eat meat maybe one day a week, and 90 percent of the time it is some sort of sausage.

Which leads me to the problem referenced above: most sausage is a way of using up pieces of meat that look better ground up, often from animals of questionable origins. If you really want to eat sausage and be healthy about it, you're going to have to make your own.

I have a meat grinder that will stuff sausage casings, but that takes a bit of time. Instead, let me share a super-easy way to make balls of sausage that you can thaw and patty for breakfast or fry for a pizza topping or otherwise use in recipes in which you want sausage to sit in for ground meat. (We used some of this on a pizza with homegrown peppers and onions and hormone-free mozzarella, sitting on a crust with flax meal and zucchini. I think that was pretty healthy.)

I bought 5 pounds of ground pork from the Amish butcher for this (so I have a better idea about how the pig was raised -- without hormones and not on a CAFO), but you can play with any ground meat you like. I occasionally use ground beef, but then I change the seasonings.

Pork Sausage
5 pounds ground pork of the best quality you can find - quality here means how the animal was raised and butchered, not necessarily which cut
5 T Tender Quick salt
5 T ground sage
5 t ground marjoram

Thaw the meat and mix with the spices and the meat cure (Tender

Quick). It is important that you buy actual meat curing salt instead of table salt -- that is what is responsible for changing the texture somewhat and curing the meat so it is better preserved.

Form into balls. I made 12 softball sized balls, so each less than a half a pound. Allow to cure 24 hours in your fridge before proceeding -- this step is important! Give that meat cure time to do its work.

Freeze, and then store in freezer bags (obviously, in the freezer). Pull one out and thaw every time you want to use sausage in your cooking.

Obviously, you can play with the seasoning mix as long as you are using the meat cure in the proportion suggested on the package. The ground sage and marjoram came from our garden, so, short of butchering the pig myself, I knew as much as I could about the origins of the ingredients in my sausage.

The Analysis

Fast: There is relatively little hands-on time with this recipe, which is good because handling meat is not my favorite thing. There is a lot of curing and thawing involved, especially if you buy your ground meat from the butcher and then freeze it until you are ready to make the sausage, which is what I did. Plan ahead. This is a great weekend activity, or you can even squeeze in the work before you leave for the office over each of a couple of mornings, as long as you plan ahead. (I actually highly recommend this. Thaw your meat overnight and make your sausage balls over about 15 minutes before you leave for work. While they cure in your fridge, walk around the office looking at your coworkers thinking "I've already made sausage this morning; what's your productivity problem?")

Cheap: Making your own sausage probably offsets the additional expense of the really good quality meat that you buy to start this recipe. With food prices going up, this may become a money-saver as well.

Good: If you are going to eat meat, I think this is the most ethical and healthy way to include sausage. Certainly, you have more control over what you are putting in your sausage and therefore what you are putting in your body. Now, to get that kind of control over our laws......

How to Roast a Whole Chicken

I tend to have this list in my head of things that I should be able to do to be called a "real housewife." I suspect a lot of us have this list, even if we don't want to admit it. Our culture has gone through a period of really devaluing the homemaking arts, and that leaves many of us (guys and gals) searching our history for touchstones that tell us if we are really doing a good job around the ole homestead. I just watched an episode of *House Hunters* on HGTV in which the young male homeowner said that he viewed buying a lawnmower as a rite of passage; to him, he had reached true homeowner status when he could go out and mow his own lawn. Presumably, a lawn service wouldn't -- pardon the pun -- cut it.

Anyway, one of the things on my list has been learning to roast a chicken. This is actually an important skill for me to learn, because our schedules depend on me and Mr. FC&G cooking something that throws off about 6 meals every Sunday. (That is, we need to feed ourselves that day, and then have leftovers for a couple of dinners and a couple of lunches for him.) Sunday is our last real opportunity to cook before Wednesday at the earliest, given that we pretty much go immediately from work to dance practice Monday and Tuesday. If there aren't ready leftovers in the fridge, we will descend quickly into grabbing junk food from the pantry on the run.

Summers are easy: Mr. FC&G will grill out a load of burgers and dogs on Sunday night, and with the garden, that is probably the cooking for the week. Winter is harder, because the garden is not there and grilling out can be miserable. Enter the chicken.

Buy your fresh chicken, open 'er up, and remove the giblets. If you are a novice, learn from one of my mistakes: **DO NOT freeze the thing on Friday and then decide on Sunday that you are in the mood to cook it after all!!** I spent over an hour thawing that thing in warm water and then prying the bag of giblets out of the cavity with my fingernail, where it was frozen to the ribs. If you buy a fresh chicken, either cook it in the next day or two, or remove the giblets to the stock bucket before you freeze it.

Anyway, once that nasty job was done, I just stuffed the cavity with onion, sage, garlic, and butter, and spread some of that yummy mix on the top. I baked it for 20 minutes for each pound, then another half hour with some Yukon Gold potatoes in with it, soaking up those drippings. I served it with biscuits and homemade preserves and some greens from the sunroom. I even made chicken gravy (drippings whisked and cooked with flour, for those of you who, like me, had to look that up).

Presto: dinner for the two of us, at least three or four lunches/dinners for Mr. FC&G, and some bones and giblets to make stock. And a much freer week for me while I try to conquer the world through my keyboard instead of in the kitchen.

The Analysis

Fast: Not fast, precisely, but certainly a low-effort thing to enjoy while sitting around on a Sunday afternoon. It takes even less time if you don't make my frozen-giblet error.

Cheap: The chicken itself comes in at less than $1 per serving, so this is the basis for a week of cheap meals.

Good: The chicken was moist and yummy, and the potatoes were to die for. Seriously, this is a homemaking skill to acquire!

5 Food Preservation

Food preservation goes hand in hand with gardening; the very nature of a garden is such that you typically have more tomatoes than you can eat in August, and a wild hunger for tomatoes the rest of the year. Your table is laden with fresh cucumbers in July but you have pickles to rely on in January. Such is the life of a gardener.

Food preservation – which includes pickling, canning, freezing, drying, and other methods – is not hard. Contemporary authors and writers make it sound like preserving your own food is comparable to splitting the atom in your kitchen, but the truth is that humans have successfully preserved food for millennia. There's no reason why you shouldn't be doing the same.

Why You Should Be Canning Your Own Food: Myths and Realities

Myth: Canning is difficult.

Fact: OK, you do have to pay attention to what you are doing, and the first few times you will feel like everything is happening at once, but very quickly you will hit a rhythm. I think canning is very relaxing, in the same way I enjoy knitting and crocheting, and others enjoy assembling model airplanes. And, just like these hobbies, you can start with something relatively easy and work your way up. I recommend starting with jam or pickles.

Myth: Home-canned food is a huge botulism danger.

Fact: I kind of blame the USDA and other typically-helpful agencies like state and county extension services, which tend to sound vaguely alarmist in their canning instructions. Botulism is certainly nothing to mess with, as it can kill, so instructions on home food preservation urge you to take every precaution.

But really, according to *Grit* magazine, there are 145 cases of botulism in the U.S. each year, about two dozen of which come from foodborne sources. And how many people are eating food in the U.S.? All but the three that are presumably on a hunger strike at any given time. Twenty-two cases divided by the U.S. population is an incredibly small risk per person. Avoiding home canning because you are afraid of botulism is like not shaking hands in this country because you are afraid of Ebola.

Myth: I can't make anything of value.

Fact: This myth burns me up, especially when I saw a recent article that predicted that interest in home canning would wane because all you can make is condiments. Yes, pickles and jams are the most common products to can, and they count as condiments. However, this overlooks the fact that almost every culture on the planet has found a way to make pickled vegetables and include them as a food source; it is our food culture that mandates that pickles are used as a slice on a burger rather than a pile on a plate. And, water bath canning is an easy method for preserving tomato chunks, sauce, and juice, none of which are condiments and all of which are dead easy to make. Finally, let's not forget the economic (and enjoyment) value of avoiding buying all those condiments in the store and instead enjoying your own.

Myth: I'll just lose money and fail spectacularly.
Fact: If you have to start your canning operations from scratch, you will not be making money the first year. You will have to buy jars, lids, a canning funnel, and a water bath canner (stock pot with rack) at minimum. However, you will reuse all of these every year except the lids, which are typically around $2 per dozen. After that first year, you will be saving money.

As far as failure, we have quite a little sub-genre of books that address the spectacular failure angle of home sustainability, supposedly to humorous results. *The $64,000 Tomato, Farm City,* and *My Empire of Dirt* are all variations on the theme of the innocent person who decides to embrace sustainability all at once and winds up investing 16 hour days and a life savings into rehabilitating a residential lot and trying to live off it. The protagonists fail or have only limited, possibly Pyrrhic, victories. No wonder people think this is hard.

Remember, though, that sustainability is all about taking one step at a time. I started gardening on my current property with only a small garden patch, and we did not pay off the mortgage from pickle savings that first year. However, I routinely take a bite out of our yearly food budget, and I make sure we have high quality, home-grown food year round. That's a sustainability victory.

Freezing Cilantro

Cilantro enjoys such a brief season. You simply must keep cutting it back, or it will flower and go to seed. Then you have a bumper crop of coriander, which is a completely different spice. The cilantro, though, you want to keep producing for all of those Latin dishes that get their unique flavor from it.

I freeze cilantro for winter use in guacamole and ropa villeja. It couldn't be easier: simply take a good size handful, chop it fine, and put it in a half pint freezer jar. Then, fill with olive oil, being sure to fill all the nooks and crannies.

That's it. Just pop it in the freezer, then thaw during those winter months when it feels like you need to head to Key West if you are ever going to get good Cuban food again. (Not that I have a problem with that approach, either, but this is cheaper.)

The Analysis

Fast: The entire process takes probably 10 minutes from harvest to freezer.

Cheap: Your only costs are the start-up costs from reusable freezer containers, and of course the olive oil. I try to use a good extra virgin olive oil, which I have discovered I can buy in bulk for cheap at a local Italian market.

Good: Since cilantro doesn't dry well, this is your only method to really ensure you have that summery flavor for Latin dishes year-round.

Freezing Cherries

We used to have a sour cherry tree. I didn't know it when we bought our property; after we had been here for a few months, my father-in-law went out back gleefully and started eating off what I was sure was a tree with ornamental berries. When he informed us we were the proud owners of a pie cherry tree, I started preserving cherries in earnest.

Alas, our cherry tree was hit by lightning. It survived one additional year, with one pathetic limb leafing out and bearing fruit, until it fell over in another storm.

Now, I purchase my cherries from the farmers' market in season, when the prices are most affordable, and I freeze them for winter use:

- Wash and pit cherries. If you plan to freeze cherries regularly, do yourself a favor and invest in a manual cherry pitter, a tool that looks a bit like a pocket on one side and a hole punch on the other. You just place the cherry in the little pocket, then close the tool to drive the spike through the cherry, taking the pit with you. If you don't have a pitter, you can do the job with a paper clip or your thumb fingernail.

- Coat the cherries in cane sugar at the rate of about 3/4 cup to a quart of cherries. You want enough to coat but not overwhelm.

- Place in storage containers, label, and freeze.

The Analysis

Fast: Pitting cherries takes some time, but I can put up about six pints in about an hour.

Cheap: No doubt these cherries are more expensive than canned prepared pie filling from the store, but they will be cheaper than the "fresh" imports from California or wherever in the middle of winter

Good: Once you make a pie with cherries you put up in summer, you'll never go back to the industrial goo covered in HFCS.

Dried Tomatoes

When people talk about food preservation, they usually talk about canning and freezing. These are two of the most entertaining, time-honored food preservation techniques, but they are also the newest. What we call canning goes back to what used to be called bottling, when homemakers would place food in glassware and seal it with fat, cloth, dough, corks, or later paraffin or canning lids. Freezing is even newer in most locales, going back primarily to Clarence Birdseye and his work in getting consumers to accept frozen foods. Prior to that, freezing really only was used in areas with naturally frozen areas, so places with permafrost or places where one could easily build an ice house, and it was not widely used for a complete range of products.

Even older, however, are cellaring and drying, both methods that control bacterial growth by using temperature or water content. Drying is one of my favorites, because it requires almost no attention, and the end product is typically much smaller than the original food to be dried, a bonus when you are storing multiple crops.

The traditional way to dry foods is to hang them on a rack or place them in a solar drier. Rack drying is great for herbs if you are processing them in small amounts, which is not true in my house; I regularly grow and store at least enough dried herbs to supply my family, my parents, and my in-laws. Solar drying, which I haven't tried, appears to work best in areas with lower humidity than the Midwest.

That leaves the electric drier as your best option. (You can use your oven on a low heat setting, but I dislike having the oven run all day.) The one I use is a $40, five-tray model from Ronco (yes, that Ronco) that I bought at the local mega-mart about five years ago. It works like a dream, and I figure since it is basically a low-wattage element at the bottom of a plastic bowl with trays on top, I should be able to keep the thing running more or less indefinitely.

One of my favorite drying projects is dried tomatoes. Dried tomatoes are one of the best products you can make in the summer, as the jars of "sundried tomatoes" are uber-expensive, and a few add a lot of flavor to dishes. I like to chop up a handful and add to pizza and pasta dishes in the fall until they are gone. There are never enough dried tomatoes.

To dry tomatoes: Select salsa-type or other fleshy tomatoes. I like drying Amish Paste and Black Krim. Wash and cut into half inch rounds. Place on dryer tray and salt with sea salt. Then put them in the drier and wait. Depending on the water content, it could take a day or two until they reach a leathery consistency; flip them periodically to hasten the drying and keep them from sticking to the tray.

Your drier does not need to run continuously; just unplug it at night or when you leave the house. Although you can store these on the shelf in oil for a while, I like the added preservation of sticking them in the freezer; they don't take up much room, and I'm even more sure I'm controlling bacterial growth. Store in a freezer container, and pull out this winter when you need a concentrated burst of summer.

The Analysis

Fast: Drying takes a while, but you don't have to participate very much. It takes me about 5 minutes to cut tomatoes for drying and then store them on the other end.

Cheap: Dried tomatoes from your garden are very low cost, depending on cost of plant (mine are typically $3 or so depending on variety, so if I get at least two dozen tomatoes per plant, I am down to about 10 cents per tomato) and amount of electricity you use in drying (minimal). By contrast, a small jar of dried tomatoes in oil is usually $3 or more.

Good: Dried tomatoes are sweet, a little smoky or deep in flavor, and a few go a long way. You really can never have enough.

Dried Lavender

I'm not much for decorative plants; one look at the petunias that I grudgingly put out each year will tell you that. However, I am in love with lavender, a rather delicate perennial that, as it turns out, is pretty useful indeed.

Many people use lavender to cook with, but I really grow it for the fragrance. I have plants out by the mailbox, where I can enjoy their scent every time I get the mail. At the end of the season, I cut all of the long-stemmed flowers and bring them inside to lay on newspapers in a sunny south-facing window. (I keep a few out for decoration in my foyer.)

Once the lavender is dry, I strip the little flower buds off and keep them in a jar. They are wonderful as potpourri; I love potpourri in my bathrooms, but I hate the neon-colored, shiny stuff you buy at the store. I also mix lavender in with my rice to make spa wraps and bed warmers for those achy muscles and cold winter nights.

The Analysis

Fast: This one takes almost no time at all. Just enjoy your lavender while it grows, then spend a few minutes total preparing it for drying and stripping the flowers when dry.

Cheap: As lavender is at least technically a perennial, the cost of the plants is spread over a few years. Mulch the plants every year to give them the best chance of coming back in the spring.

Good: Nothing smells better than lavender in a bed warmer!

Dried Oregano Blossoms

One of the best parts of gardening is being able to select your fruits, veggies, and herbs at the stage at which you like them best -- if you love green tomatoes or baby zucchini, they are there for you without the need to pay a premium price.

One of the luxuries I like is dried oregano blossoms to use as the herb oregano in lieu of just using the leaves. The blossoms, picked just before they open into a pretty white flower, have a really intense oregano flavor and smell, even when dried. You can bet that isn't usually one of your options on the grocery spice rack!

The Analysis

Fast: Pick a few stems, rinse, and pop them in the food dehydrator; in a few hours, you have concentrated herb goodness!

Cheap: Drying food and herbs is one of the cheapest methods of preservation out there. To maximize the electricity used with an electric dehydrator, I try to make sure I have at least 3 of the 5 trays full.

Good: If you are growing oregano this year, try saving some of the blossoms. You'll be pleasantly surprised at the intensity.

WWII Chili Sauce

August is undeniably tomato month, and I like to use the bounty to put up some of our favorite winter meal solutions. One of these is affectionately known as "WWII Chili Sauce."

This recipe derives its name from its origins in *Grandma's Wartime Kitchen* by Joanne Lamb Hayes. Although Hayes has devised a way to make this sauce in about a half hour of cook time, I am going against the "Fast" of "Fast, Cheap, and Good" by reverse engineering it to cook longer, making for a thicker sauce and deeper flavors. It is worth the investment of time.

Mr. FC&G loves this sauce. On a cold winter night that he is cooking for himself, I can assist by thawing a pound of hamburger and letting him use this like sloppy joe sauce. It makes a great topping for bread, noodles, or potatoes, and it makes about 4-5 servings of sloppy joe-style chili.

3 lb. tomatoes
1/2 cup chopped onions
1/2 cup chopped pepper (use green peppers for a mild taste, or hot chilies for spice)
1/4 cup cider vinegar
1/4 cup packed light brown sugar
1/2 t. salt
1/4 t. ground cloves
1/4 t. ground allspice

Wash and stem the tomatoes, cutting into reasonable size chunks and cutting out bad spots. Place in large pot and cook until the tomatoes are juicy and boiling. The longer you cook, the more juice and pulp will be available to you.

When the tomatoes have released their juice, pass the juice and pulp through a ricer (also called a food mill) to remove the skins and seeds. Return the tomato pulp to the pan, and add the remaining ingredients. Return to a gentle boil, and cook until the sauce is as thick as you would like – depending on the tomatoes you have used and the size of the batch, this could take up to 2 hours.

Refrigerate for use within a week, or spoon into a sterilized pint jar, leaving 1/4-1/2 inch headspace, and process in a water bath canner for 20 minutes (25 minutes for quarts). Makes one pint.

The Analysis

Fast: Well, I did make the cook time longer on this by virtue of cooking the pulp down, sending it through a ricer, and then cooking again. I think it is worth it.

Cheap: Depending on your garden, this could be quite cheap indeed, with the cost coming mostly or entirely from pantry supplies (like cider vinegar and spices).

Good: Once you've had this, I promise the sticky, HFCS-laden sloppy joe sauce in a can will hold very little appeal for you. And, as a bonus, the house smells wonderful while you cook it!

Homemade Ketchup

Making your own ketchup is one of those homemaker stunts that
seems impossibly hard core, kind of like making cheese. But both of
these processes are actually pretty easy -- with an edge to ketchup,
because you can put it on the stove and forget it while it cooks down
and you do something else.

1 6-oz can tomato paste (go ahead and splurge on organic, because
this is worth doing "right")
2 T white vinegar (you can use cider vinegar in a pinch, but don't
omit, because this make it safe to can)
1 T brown sugar
1 t molasses
1 t garlic powder
1 t onion powder
1/4 t allspice
1 t salt
1 can water (rinse out all the remaining tomato paste with this)

Combine ingredients in sauce pan. Cook until desired consistency,
which should take about 20 minutes for this amount. If you desire a
longer cook time to better blend the flavors, add more water at the
beginning and cook down.

Pour into glass jars and store in fridge. It will keep for a few months,
but don't let it languish for a year like you might do with store
versions that contain preservatives.

If you choose to can it, double or triple the batch; or go even further
and get the super-big cans of tomato paste to put up several jars.
(This batch makes just over a half pint.) Can in half pint jars; if you
are a single person household or a family that doesn't eat a lot of
ketchup, consider canning in the half-cup jelly jars. Process in a water
bath canner for 20 minutes. Cool and store.

The Analysis

Fast: I cooked a double batch in about 25 minutes, exactly the amount of time it took me to frost and decorate a cake for a family party. If you choose to can a batch, it will be a bit longer, but this is a great mid-winter canning project since it doesn't depend on fresh veggies.

Cheap: Catch a sale on organic tomato paste, and this will be way cheaper than store ketchup. Not to mention, you won't have to read the label to make sure there is no HFCS.

Good: Mr. FC&G and I like the flavor of this much better than store-bought. It is a bit deeper and more nuanced. And, of course, I get serious homemaker cred for making my own ketchup!

Sauce from Frozen Tomatoes

The best thing about growing tomatoes is making sauce and juice, filling the kitchen with the warm smells of tomato-y goodness. The worst thing, probably, is that in a good tomato year, you are likely to be cooking and canning several quarts of tomato sauce in August, just when you least want to be warming up the kitchen.

Several friends recommended that I try freezing my sauce tomatoes and cooking them in winter, and I tried it. Even though most paste tomato varieties (which make the best sauce) are determinate, meaning that they are bred to fruit all at once, I still find that there is a spread of a few weeks over which the Amish Paste, Ukrainian Purple, and Ox Heart tomatoes will ripen. As it was such a miserable tomato year for me, I would find myself with a couple of ripe paste tomatoes at a time, but rarely enough for a batch of sauce.

So I took everyone's advice. I washed the paste tomatoes as they ripened, then cut off the stem end and any blemishes, and put them straight into a freezer bag. There they sat, accumulating little tomato buddies slowly, until the end of the season.

Over Christmas, I finally pulled them out and used them to make a small batch of sauce. They performed wonderfully. Because the freezing softens the tomatoes a bit (due to breaking down cell walls), they cooked up more quickly, and it was easier to extract the "meat" of the tomato with my ricer. The resulting sauce was yummy, with no noticeable difference between this batch and the fresh-cooked batch I made over the summer. I'm officially a convert; I will be freezing my paste tomatoes for cooler weather processing from now on!

The Analysis

Fast: This batch of sauce arguably cooked up faster than it would have with fresh tomatoes over the summer. But the big difference is moving the hot cooking process into a month it does me some good.

Cheap: One could make an argument that the tomatoes required energy to be frozen until processing, compared with sitting in their jars as sauce over that period. However, the freezer is running anyway, and I'm sure any additional energy it took to cool the tomatoes down was much less than the energy it takes to run the AC non-stop during one of those hot August nights of sauce-canning. The only downfall is a bit of risk -- if a major power outage had occurred, I would have potentially lost the tomatoes if they had not yet been turned into sauce. However, I note that I'm not above cooking a batch of sauce on the cookstove or the backyard grill if I have to.

Good: Equal quality to those processed in summer!

Homemade Apple Sauce

You have to love the farmer's market. When I asked my favorite fruit farm owner about the best apples for sauce, the lady asked me how much I wanted to put up, then offered to bring me a half bushel of seconds for a lower price. Seconds are definitely the way to go for sauce; since you don't need pretty, unblemished apples, you can take ones with small bruises and irregular forms for a lower price. She brought me a half bushels of mixed varieties of apples, and I paid $18. True to my requested estimate, this was enough to put up 12 pints of homemade applesauce.

I loved this project, because I could control the sugar and spice, generating a great end product. I also tried putting up some apple jelly made with the cores; it didn't set quite as well as I might have liked, but this is never a problem in this house. Loose jams and jellies are yogurt and coffee flavorings, or pancake and ice cream topping. No waste here!

Mixed apples
Sugar
Cinnamon
Nutmeg

1. Wash the apples very well. I washed them with a dishcloth under running water. Even organic farms will have to do some spraying and pest control, so you don't want any residue, even if it is a natural product.

2. Core the apples and cut into chunks. Here's a tip from my friend: don't peel them. Boil them until they are soft, and the peels will slip right off. Run the apples through a ricer, which will remove the remaining skins, seeds, or other nasty parts. The sauce will be the only thing making it through the holes of the ricer.

3. Reheat the sauce until nearly boiling, adding sugar and spices to taste. I used about a half a cup of sugar for 2.5 quarts of sauce, along with about 2 t. cinnamon and 1/2 t. nutmeg. What you use depends on your apples and your taste. I canned multiple small batches

instead of one big batch because Mr. FC&G and I were working assembly-line fashion.

4. Can in pint or quart jars, according to your family's need. Leave about 3/4 inch headspace. For either size, process for 20 minutes in a boiling water canning bath.

The Analysis

Fast: Putting up a half bushel of apples took about 3-4 hours, including the jelly experiment. Like so many things this time of year, a good evening of canning turns into good food for an entire year.

Cheap: Just figuring the sauce, my apple costs were 10.6 cents per ounce of sauce in 2011, and I spent about $22 total on apples, sugar, spices, and pectin for the sauce plus six 12-ounce jars of "jelly." I haven't bought store applesauce in years, but I imagine this compares very favorably.

Good: The best part of this project is customizing the applesauce to your own taste. I can hardly wait to crack open one of these jars and have applesauce as part of my lunches.

6 Textiles

Think you can't sew and therefore can't do anything sustainable regarding clothing and household textiles? Think again. There are many ways to avoid waste and live more sustainably with some easy no- and low-sew textile projects.

I'm not a tremendous seamstress. My most ambitious projects run to fleece socks and nightshirts and flannel PJ pants – nothing that requires a lot of skill. Nonetheless, I'm able to handle the basics to complete some of the projects I want to do, saving money and resources along the way. This chapter should give you some ideas of things you can do, too.

Ersatz Cotton Balls

I have a fleece addiction.

Let me back up a bit. In the course of my sustainable living journey, I try to find sustainable replacements for the kind of disposable items that are so annoying to pay for. For me, one of these is cotton balls.

I know, I know. They aren't that expensive. But cotton balls are one of those inherently disposable items that slowly leach money from your wallet while they add to the landfill. So, since I use cotton balls primarily as makeup removers, enter the ersatz cotton ball.

This requires another slight digression: I love the remnant fabric bin at my local fabric store, and winter is the time that this bin is filled with fleece. After everyone spent Christmas making homemade Snuggies, that bin is full of miscuts, unwanted yardage, and the ends of bolts. So, if you aren't ultra-picky about the patterns you buy (and make no mistake, there are some cute ones and some wonderful solids in there), you can usually pick up fleece remnants ranging up to a yard and a half in length, all for 50 to 70 percent off.

I have been raiding the remnant bin for months to find pieces with which to make fleece socks, so I happened to have some white fleece ends left over, but any color would do. Simply cut your fleece remnant into 2"x2" squares, and there you have it -- make up remover pads, otherwise known as ersatz cotton balls. Fleece doesn't fray, so you don't have to worry about hemming, which makes this a fine no-sew project.

I hang a mesh laundry bag on the back of the bathroom door, and when I have a reasonable bag full of dirties, I toss them in the white load. I don't up the amount of detergent I use, and the weight of these is so negligible that I don't think my machine is adding more than a few cents' extra water. In the summer, I hang that mesh bag out on the clothes line to dry, so they dry for free. Best of all, I can use these again and again.

The Analysis

Fast: I think it took me 10 minutes to make a jar full of ersatz cotton balls, enough to last me a while. On a busy grocery day, it could take me that long to slog my way down the make-up aisle to get cotton balls.

Cheap: I raided my own fleece stash and used pieces too small for anything else, but assuming you buy light-colored fleece for this project, you should be able to make all you need for about a quarter of a yard. If you get your yardage from the remnant bin, you should not be spending more than 50 cents to a dollar.

Good: I would say these are just as soft or softer than cotton balls, and they remove makeup just as well. Plus, they last forever: some of the original batch I made lasted well over three years.

Fleece Pillowcases

In the winter, I sew and do textile crafts for relaxation; in the summer, I garden. And as I have mentioned, I am in love with the remnant rack at our local fabric store.

An easy project to undertake is the fleece pillowcase. It requires only two seams and a hem, so it is very easy to complete if you have a sewing machine, and it is oh-so soft and cozy on a winter night.

For this project, I lucked into a beautiful piece of remnant fleece that was a yard and quarter long, but you really only need a scrap that is two-thirds of a yard in length. Most fleece comes in 58 inch widths, so that is perfect for covering a standard pillow.

Step 1: Cut your fabric.

Leave the 58 inch "width" intact and cut the "length" of the remnant. I cut mine to about 21 inches; you may wish to cut yours a little longer if you have extra-puffy pillows, as this measurement will make the width of the pillowcase. Don't go too far overboard, though, because too much fabric will make a baggy pillowcase.

Fold the fabric in half lengthwise, so the 58 inch side of the fabric (which is the width of the fleece on the bolt, but is the length of the pillowcase; this is confusing to read but will make more sense with a piece of fabric in your hand) is doubled. Make sure right sides of the fabric are together. You will see that the part that will become the bottom edge of the pillowcase is already made by the fold; you just have two side seams to do in order to make a bag, which is all a pillowcase really is.

Step 2: Sew up side seams.

Sew each side seam with 3/8 inch seam allowance. This isn't set in stone; it is just a sewing convention I was taught. More or less seam allowance will make the pillowcase tighter or looser, so here is where you can make up for a mistake in cutting if needed. Lock in your stitches at the top and bottom of the seam.

Step 3: Sew the hem.

Fold the raw edges of the opening down an inch. Make sure you are folding toward the wrong side of the fabric, which should still be the side of the fabric you see. Since fleece doesn't fray, you don't have to fold in twice as you would with other fabrics. Sew the hem with a zig-zag stitch.

Step 4: Turn the pillowcase right side out.
You are done!

The Analysis

Fast: This project routinely takes me a half an hour; it may take you a bit longer if you are a novice sewer.

Cheap: Definitely. Take advantage of that remnant bin. I got a yard and a quarter of this fabric for $4.63, and I used about two-thirds of a yard. That works out to $2.44 for fabric costs. Throw a few cents on for thread, and you arrive at $2.50. You cannot buy a standard pillowcase in any fabric for that amount.

Good: My hubby raves about these in the winter months; they are so soft and warm. I think they are one of those little touches that make it that much easier to turn down the heat at night and cozy up, listening to the sweet sound of the heat not running and money not being spent.

Reusable Duster Mop Cloths

The good folks at Swiffer were really onto something when they created the Swiffer mop. Sure, there had been other mops that could be used to dust or scrub, depending on the amount of liquid you used, but the Swiffer mop had one feature I'd never encountered before: that universal joint that attaches the handle to the head. It gives me the most delicious feeling of "hey, I'm mopping the floors really fast!" (I know, I need to get out more.) It also reaches into corners and around round things in ways you wouldn't expect from a blocky rectangle head. I've worn mine until the handle is about to snap.

What I don't love is the disposable cloths that you use once, throw out, and buy again and again. Part of me wants to make a high-minded argument to you that it is not environmentally responsible to keep buying cardboard boxes and plastic tubs full of dust cloths and floor washing cloths, only to send them to a landfill about 2 minutes after you use it. But the whiner in me was just really tired of paying for the things, lugging them home, and then lugging them to the curb later (OK, hubby does that last part, but you get the point.)

Enter the fleece substitute. As you may know, I can solve anything with fleece. It is the duct tape of fabrics, and right now there are many remnants of fleece -- bolt ends and miscuts -- in a bin at your local fabric store. Go get a remnant for less than you would pay for a single box of refills (I regularly get about a yard for less than $2 in the remnant bin), and cut into about 6" by 10" rectangles. They fit onto the head beautifully. Spray with whatever cleaning fluid you like, or none; the fleece does a great job of dusting. Then just wash them with sheets, towels, jeans, or whatever heavy-duty load you have.

(As an aside, as an instructor of advertising history, I am fascinated by the number of products that are currently sold with the message "use once and throw the dirt/germs away." It will be interesting to see how this evolves as our societal germ-phobia comes up against the increasing interest in sustainability.)

The Analysis

Fast: Not counting time for a trip to the fabric store (because that's pleasure, right?), a stack of these took about 10 minutes to cut. I wasn't particularly exact about it.

Cheap: I made a stack of these for less than $1. I still purchase the disposable wet cloths occasionally, but I might purchase one box in a calendar year, compared to probably one every six weeks plus a nearly comparable amount of the disposable dusting cloths before I started making these reusable ones. Let's do the math on this one, using 2010 prices:

Before reusable cloths:
9 boxes wet cloths per year @ $5.09 ea. (Costco) = $45.81
6 boxes dry cloths per year @ $4.42 ea. (Amazon) = $26.52
Total = $72.33

With reusable cloths:
Stack of fleece reusable cloths = $1
1 box wet cloths = $5.09
Total = $6.09

Savings: $66.24 for about 10 minutes of work

Good: They work just as well as the commercial variety, and you will use them again and again!

Wash Cloths from Ruined Towels

I once cherished (and accidentally got published in *Reader's Digest*, but that's another story) a quote that said, "Practice doesn't make perfect, nor is it supposed to. Practice is about increasing your repertoire of ways to recover from your mistakes." Nowhere is this as true as in homemaking.

When Mr. FC&G and I were first married, I got distracted doing laundry, and I bleached a towel that should not have been bleached. I then retired the towel to dirty jobs like highlighting hair, which means that over the years it has taken additional bleach damage. The result was a towel with intermittent bleach spots and a few holes.

Now, the obvious choice is to turn the towel into rags, but I thought I'd see what I could salvage. I was able to cut seven 12"x12" wash cloths out of the good parts of the towel, still leaving several cleaning rags.

The raw edges I finished by turning them under a half an inch and sewing with a zig-sag stitch. Note that not all edges of a cloth need to be finished; the ones that originally were the bottom and sides of the towel are fine as they are.

Did I need to do this? No. However, I took some pleasure in saving an item that I had destroyed with my carelessness. And, when you look at it, I saved a little money:

The Analysis:

Fast: I tend to sew simple things as thought breaks while I work, so putting these cloths on the pile to be finished didn't really take much additional time out of my schedule.

Cheap: The least expensive wash cloth of any significant weight I can find in the store is $1, and I have seen heavy ones go for as much as $5 a piece. Since I was able to get seven cloths out of my destroyed towel, I in effect created $7 worth of value. I doubt the original towel cost more than $7 (many years ago at a discount department store), so I have either saved money I would otherwise have spent on new washcloths, or at minimum I have preserved the value of the original towel.

Good: This one comes down to a philosophy of waste. If you look at your mistakes and think "how can I recover from that and respect the resource given to me," then you will over time save money and cultivate a more respectful attitude toward the things you work so hard to buy.

Achoo! Homemade Hankies

I love Spring: the ground is warming, the birds are singing, the plants and trees are flowering....

Uh oh. I mean, "achoo!" Sometimes I think Ohio has two seasons: hypothermia, and allergy/asthma. We are firmly in the latter, and, in previous years, this has meant a real boon for the facial tissue companies.

In a month of allergy season, we can go through about four boxes of tissues around here. At $1.35 a pop for the store brand, this adds up. So, I've switched about 90% of my tissue usage to hankies.

I am aware of the standard complaint that hankies let you carry your germs with you; the solution, of course, is to have enough hankies to toss in the wash frequently. They wash up with any number of loads, so you should never have to run a special hankie load. And making them is a snap. Try one of the below methods:

Method One: Hankies to be Seen in Public
Take soft, used cotton and cut a square about 12" by 12" (bigger or smaller according to preference). I have made some lovely hankies out of an old jumper that looked horrid on me but was made from a wonderful fabric. Turn each side under a half inch twice (that is, turn it under a half inch, then turn that under another half inch). Run a zig-zag or straight seam up the fold, or whip stitch by hand. Embroider if you wish.

Method Two: Hankies for Household Use
This is my favorite: cut old t-shirts and tank tops to your preferred size. Since t-shirt material doesn't fray, you don't have to seam them. And since no one will see them but your housemates, who cares what they look like? And how pretty does something have to be to be more attractive than a used tissue?

The Analysis

Fast: Method One is for those looking for a craft project. Method Two is for those who need hankies -- and lots of them -- in a hurry. I can cut a t-shirt apart in a couple of minutes. Obviously, you can cut around any stains and get some extra life out of those garments, too.

Cheap: Well-worn material makes the softest hankies, and it is free. If you are feeling miserly doing this, think of it as "aged and distressed to make a soft finished product." If I avoid buying three of my usual four monthly boxes of tissues, I save $4.05 a month during allergy season.

Good: I actually find soft cotton to be easier on skin than tissues, and it certainly creates less waste and expense.

Bed Warmers, AKA "Knee Thingies"

In many spa-related stores, you can find little bags filled with buckwheat or other materials designed to be heated or chilled for your therapeutic and relaxation pleasure. These delightful little bags are often called "bed warmers" because they can be heated in the microwave and used to keep the foot of your bed warm for hours; they are also called "spa wraps" if you make a longer version that can be either heated or chilled to wrap around shoulders or sore muscles. Since the most common use of these in our household is to soothe my bad knee, they are called "knee thingies" around here.

To make one, choose your favorite scrap of cozy fabric. I used a leftover piece of flannel from a pair of PJ pants I made, but you can use anything you love. In fact, I encourage you to use a piece that makes you smile when you see it; I made one last year using a piece of buffalo plaid from a 1980s dress I had, and I love seeing that fabric every time I use it.

You are just making a pillow. Sew up three and a half sides of your fabric (with right sides together), and turn your bag inside out. You should have a gap about half the width of the short side through which to fill the bag.

Mix your filling. For a small one about the size of a piece of notebook paper, I used about 2 cups of rice and 2/3 cup of lavender blossoms. You want to let the filling be pretty slack, so it conforms to your feet, knee, or wherever you like. I used a canning funnel in the opening of my bag to fill it with the rice and lavender mixture. You can use any spice or herb; cinnamon and nutmeg are nice too.

Sew up the opening. You can whip it by hand; I used a zig-zag stitch on my sewing machine. You want to use a stitch you can pick out, because you really want to empty and change the filling once in a while (although I really have been bad about this). The filling is compostable, and then the bag itself is washable if you used a washable fabric.

To chill, put the bag in the freezer. We keep one there most of the time, wrapped in a couple of plastic grocery bags to ward off freezer funk. They are wonderful for post-exercise knee pain. To heat, put in the microwave. I nuke mine for about 3-4 minutes on high depending on size; you will want to experiment with your own particular bag and microwave. Stick close the first few times; I have never had a problem, but you want to exercise the caution appropriate to putting a cloth bag of grain into the microwave.

The Analysis

Fast: I can whip a "knee thingie" up in about 20 minutes.

Cheap: My only expense was a couple of cups of cheap rice. The lavender was from my garden, and the fabric was a remnant.

Good: If you haven't experienced sliding one of these into the foot of your bed on a cold night, you are in for a treat. In spite of my reticence to turn on the heat, I am fundamentally a person who can't maintain body heat, and one of these will keep me warm most of the night. I actually like to have the bedroom a little cold just so I can enjoy the weight of a pile of quilts and the warmth of a "knee thingie."

Hand Warmers

These little gems are a small-sized version of bed warmers, just for your pockets. I took two 4.5 inch squares of fleece per hand warmer, sewed them up like a pillow, then filled with rice and spice (a rhyme, no less!). One pair I filled with rice and sage, which made my pockets smell a bit like Thanksgiving stuffing; as I've mentioned before, lavender and cinnamon/cloves are also nice additions.

Microwave these for a minute and slide them in your coat pockets for a little bit of warmth while you are out in the cold. I actually wound up walking to my destination one 20 degree day, and my hands remained toasty on the entire trip thanks to these little guys.

They are a great last-minute Christmas gift, as they will fit right in a stocking.

The Analysis

Fast: I sewed and filled a pair in about 20 minutes. Since they were for me, I seemed the top with the machine; if you are giving them as a gift, you may want to hand sew the top with blind stitch, which will take a little longer.

Cheap: Fleece from the remnant bin, homegrown sage, and bulk rice -- these are literally pennies a piece.

Good: Warm hands made a mile and a half walk pleasant in cold weather.

Fleece Patchwork "(Un)quilt"

(Note: As of this writing, this is the most popular post on my blog, consistently ranking number one and always boasting a boost in hits when fall comes and people are looking for easy ways to make blankets for themselves or gifts. I have made two for our home and one for a gift, so you know they are easy!)

I am in love with this fleece patchwork quilt pattern, which is really quick and easy because there is no actual quilting involved -- that is, there is no batting between the layers and no top stitching. Therefore, it might best be called a fleece blanket, but I like the idea of calling it an (un)quilt.

You already know of my love for the remnant bin at my favorite fabric store. The prices there are amazing; bolt ends and miscuts are sold at whatever that day's sale is on the fabric, plus 50% off for remnants. I can regularly score a yard of fabric for around $2.

For this project, all you need are remnants in fleece patterns and colors you like, plus a cut of fleece for backing. Follow these simple steps:

1. Cut the patchwork fleece into squares. I use a 4.5 inch square quilting template because I like the look of random patches of regularly-cut fabric. But feel free to get more complex or to try patterns like a 9-patch square. Just remember that the more complex your patchwork, the more time it takes.

2. Sew your squares together. For me, I sew 14 squares to get the width; this is about five feet in width. I like this width for a fleece quilt because bolts of fleece come in 58-60 inch widths, so this will fit the backing without piecing two cuts of fleece together to make the back. That is difficult and unwieldy. Five feet wide also allows me to put the quilt on my side of the (king) bed without disturbing over-heated hubby.

3. Sew your width strips together to make about six feet in length. Again, six feet is two yards of fleece, which is an inexpensive backing. Alternately, you could patch the back as well, but that would be more work.

4. For the back, buy a piece of fleece two yards long and about 60 inches wide. Place the backing and the topper with right sides together and machine sew on three sides, like you are making a pillow case. For the fourth side (which would be open on a pillow case), turn the edges in and sew both sides together. You can do this on your machine (remember, that is four thicknesses of fabric, so you may want to change to a heavier needle) or by blind stitch. Sometimes, I use a piece of blanket binding to bind the "open" fourth side together instead.

Voila! A soft, warm "quilt" that really relies on the warmth of air sandwiched in two layers of fleece instead of the normal cotton and batting sandwich. If you are crafty, you could easily sew one of these up as a Christmas gift (a lap quilt also would be nice and take even less time), or you could start one to keep your own toes toasty in the bitter months to come.

The Analysis

Fast: In quilt-time, this one comes together in a jiffy. Cut squares while you are watching TV at night, and then sew together in a few bursts of sewing. I like to work on one of these while I'm writing, because it gives me a chance to turn away from the computer and think for a few minutes while I assemble a few squares.

Cheap: I put my first fleece quilt together for the cost of $14 for two yards of backing fleece, plus whatever I spent on remnants. You should be able to bring this project in under $30 with some smart shopping.

Good: The fleece quilt is one of the (very) few things I actually like about winter. It is so soft and warm, it follows me everywhere: downstairs onto the couch during the day, and upstairs onto the bed at night. I can't wait to finish another.

7 Household Helps

Early housekeeping manuals always had a section called "household helps," a section that persisted in cookbooks at least up to the 1960s. This section will introduce some of my little tips and tricks that help our house run more smoothly and help us save money, time, and resources.

Snow-Washing Rugs

I am no fan of winter. I am so eager to go south that I grow a dwarf key lime tree, letting it live outside during the warm months and bringing it in to a south-facing window in winter, where we both look longingly out, searching for sun.

However, there is one thing that you can do in winter that meets our trifecta of fast, cheap, and good. (Well, two things, but the other one really shouldn't be all that fast....) You can snow-wash your wool (and other fiber) rugs.

Cleaning wool throw rugs is problematic, because you can't always vacuum them completely clean, and they don't wash well. So, you are often forced to use a spray or sprinkle carpet cleaner, which just introduces unnecessary chemicals into your house.

A better solution is snow-washing, the traditional technique for cleaning rugs from before the era of vacuum cleaners. Nothing could be easier:

1. Wait for a snowfall. A fairly cold snow is best; a good packing snow has a tendency to pack itself right onto the rug, making it a little too wet.

2. Take your wool rugs outside and turn upside down in clean snow.

3. Beat out your frustrations on the backs of those rugs. I have a rug beater because I actually clean rugs with it, but you can get the same result using a clean broom.

4. Pick your rugs up. If you have really waited a while between cleanings, you will be rewarded with a spot of dirt in the snow where the rug once was. The snow flakes and granules have worked their way into the rug and scrubbed gently on their way out, removing the dirt.

5. Shake off the excess snow and lay the rug flat in the house in a place it can dry. A basement or foyer with a hard surface floor is perfect, as you don't want any residual snow melting onto other carpets.

6. Return to its place when dry.

The Analysis

Fast: Yes. I feel this strategy is actually faster than spraying on a chemical and dragging out the vacuum to sweep.

Cheap: Yes, this one is my favorite kind of cheap: free. You just wait for Mother Nature to provide a snowfall.

Good: I think so. The rugs get clean without introducing chemicals into your home at a time when your home is likely closed up and less ventilated anyway. You even burn a few calories and work out some frustrations in the process of beating.

Fall Linen Washing

One of my traditional fall tasks, regardless of the temperature or duration of Indian Summer, is to wash all of the quilts, bedspreads, and blankets and hang them on the outside line to dry. This simple tip allows you to start your winter with bedding and throws that all smell of summer, and, for me, every quilt I hang to dry saves me about an hour of drier time. I typically do this every October.

One caveat: October has less heat, less direct sunlight, and shorter days than, say, July. In July, I can pretty much do this task (if I wish -- I usually do it in May to prepare for summer) in one July day by continually washing quilts and knowing they will be dry in about two hours. In October, each quilt takes all day to dry, so plan ahead and prioritize your loads to take advantage of the few remaining warm days ahead!

The Analysis

Fast: Line drying is definitely slower than using the appliance, but you don't really have to be involved for much of the process, either way.

Cheap: As noted, for me each quilt washed and line-dried saves about an hour of drier time. I'm not sure what this translates to in dollars and cents, but it has to be noticeable.

Good: Your bonus is fresh bedding that smells of sun and fresh air to cuddle into during the cold weeks to come.

Steam-Cleaning the Shower

One job I really despise is cleaning the shower. There are few jobs worse, in my opinion, than scrubbing off dirt and soap scum in a damp, confined space. Add to this the expense of cleaners, which typically come in an ecological nightmare of a container made of metal and plastic and containing a mix of noxious chemicals and propellants, and this job is pretty low on my list.

Now, in the interest of full disclosure, I must admit that I do occasionally use those expensive cleaners. For all their lung-burning faults, they do tend to loosen the scum enough to clean it off. However, to reduce the use of those chemicals, we use a steam cleaner to clean our shower. Mr. FC&G typically does this job.

Steamers are a great way to clean bathrooms. They heat and direct a burst of steam at whatever you are cleaning, and ours came with a variety of attachments that let you scrub or scrape or otherwise direct the flow of steam. Although the initial investment in the equipment will typically set you back around $100 (our unit was a gift from my folks), they require only electricity and water after that, and you get sanitized surfaces with no chemical fumes or residue. (Warning: Although you can use your steamer to clean in and around your toilet, don't direct a long-term burst of steam at the gap where the toilet meets the floor, because you could accidentally melt the wax washer if you heat it up too much. However, a quick run around that area is enough to get the job done and won't harm anything.)

Now, these steamers are not perfect solutions to the cleaning dilemma, as they do take time to set up and heat up. However, if we do a super-good cleaning of the shower once a month with the steamer and then are diligent about rinsing the shower down once a day with the hand-held shower head (I do this after my shower each day), we have a pretty clean shower, and we only occasionally resort to the canned chemical cocktail to get the job done.

The Analysis

Fast: Using a steamer is nowhere near as fast as spraying a burst of foam at the problem, but it certainly does a better job. This is a moderately big cleaning job that takes some time.

Cheap: Once you have the equipment, you are talking about pennies of electricity and water per use. You should eventually recoup your investment
in foregone chemical cleaners. The more you use it, the faster it pays itself off.

Good: Perhaps the best part of the process is knowing that you have a sanitized shower with no chemical fumes or residue.

Cutting Costs with Coupons, Carefully

If one of your primary motivations for embracing sustainability is saving money (and good for you, if so), then you will have found numerous books and blogs advising you to clip coupons. If you watch daytime television, you have no doubt flipped on a show featuring some consumer who has managed to get her weekly groceries for free thanks to some fortuitous combination of coupons, coupon doubling, store sales, and rebates.

If you are like me, after you deal with your feelings of coupon inadequacy, you start wondering what this woman is feeding her family. If I actually could pull off a stunt like this, something tells me I would have a cart full of kids' yogurt and toaster pastries, plus 117 packages of disposable razors. You will notice that the best sales always come on items that are full of HFCS, are overly-processed, or are headed for a landfill after use.

Processed food and consumer product companies know that the small sales promotion known as a coupon will bring in those of us trying to save money; they hope it will gain them a convert to their product. But be aware, they don't really want to let you have something for nothing.

One night, I made my way out during a winter storm for an appointment, and along the way I stopped at the grocery. (Names omitted to protect the guilty.) I had in my hands a recent sales promotion for a premium brand of coffee offering a "free pound of coffee, up to $4.00." Naturally, this is something I wanted to take advantage of.

Well, the store didn't post the price per pound, and I wasn't as vigilant as I should have been. (This is thanks in part to the 20 minutes I spent digging my car out of the snow drift I call a driveway, but I digress.) The end result was that I wound up with a pound of coffee listed at $7 and change per pound, for which I had a $4 coupon. Still a respectable discount, but nothing to write home about price-wise.

My lesson? If you are going to play the coupon game, remember that the deck is stacked in favor of the house, and it takes a great deal of planning to truly score a coupon deal. I can't grow coffee, and I will drink this, so it is a fairly cheap lesson. Had I purchased a food I could grow or make for myself and had a similar situation occur, I would be extremely angry.

The Analysis

Fast: Coupons require time to clip, organize, and coordinate with your grocery list and store sales. Only clip coupons for items and specific brands you would buy anyway, at full price.

Cheap: Not necessarily. It is not at all out of the question for there to be a temporary price hike, either by the manufacturer or the store, that offsets your coupon. Again, a coupon is only a deal if you would have purchased the item anyway. If the coupon is the deciding factor, put the item back.

Good: Make it your goal to try to restrict the food portions of your grocery list to the elements of food, rather than processed food, and you will see that your food bill goes down and that there are very few coupons available for you anyway. Coupons for flour, spices, meat, and veggies are few and far between

Buy Baking Supplies at the Holidays

Baking supplies tend to go on sale around the major "cooking holidays," like Christmas, Thanksgiving, and Easter. As each holiday approaches, check your store for specials on flour, powdered sugar, brown sugar, yeast, and spices. Many of these will be displayed on the end caps of the aisles. I tend to buy store brands of most things, but if you prefer brand name spices (which I do for ones I don't grow), there is usually a coupon or two to be had in the weeks leading up to the holidays. Since these baking supplies tend to keep for months or longer, this is a smart time to pick up an extra bag of brown sugar or an extra jar of yeast.

The Analysis

Fast: Obviously, it takes no more time to buy an item on sale than it does to buy one full price. I'll give you that it takes a few extra seconds to carry that second bag of brown sugar to the cart and then in from the car....

Cheap: Stocking up on basic supplies when they go on predictable sales is an easy and smart money management technique.

Good: Having the right cooking supplies on hand, purchased at a good price, is a great incentive to cook more of your own meals and treats at home.

Homemade Laundry Soap

Making your own laundry soap sounds like one of those hard-core cheap-o things to do that only the fanatics among us would attempt. Once I started making my own, however, I found that it is amazingly easy, astoundingly cheap, and cleans my laundry better than store-bought detergents.

You will need:

One bar pink Zote soap. This is a laundry soap formulated for easy grating and good cleaning and brightening.
1 1/2 cup baking soda
1 1/2 cup borax
(Note: These amounts will make enough to fill an old one quart yogurt container.)

Grate a third of a bar of Zote into a bowl. Zote is a very soft soap that grates easily with a vegetable grater. Keep the bar well wrapped so it doesn't dry out between uses, as the harder soap is more difficult to grate.

Add baking soda and borax, and mix. Store.

You will use only about two teaspoons per load, so this stuff lasts forever. Experiment until you find the right amount for your washer, but don't overdo. Excess soap will lay in the soap tray if you overload it, so start with a teaspoon and work your way up, especially if you have a high efficiency washer.

I started using this just on towels, then moved on to underwear, jeans, and finally all of my laundry. (Full disclosure: I "treat" my black laundry to a special dark fabrics detergent, even though I've never noticed my homemade soap causing any fading.) Hubby notes that workout clothes washed in the homemade variety don't smell "sour" after wearing, like they do with commercial detergents. Plus, I think the clothes look cleaner, and they definitely smell outdoor clean without having a perfume smell.

The Analysis

Fast: It takes about 10-15 minutes to make a batch of laundry soap. Not a big investment in time to save a lot of money!

Cheap: I knew this was inexpensive, but I didn't realize how cheap until I did the math:

Zote: One bar is $0.99, so a third of a bar is $0.33.

Baking Soda: A 64 oz. box is $1.99, so a cup and a half is $0.37.

Borax: A 76 oz. box of 20 Mule Team Borax is $3.99, so a cup and a half is $0.63.

Total: $1.33 for a full quart container of laundry soap.

Good: Cleaner, better smelling clothes, no detergents in the waste water stream, no big empty plastic bottles in the landfill (recycle those cardboard baking soda and borax boxes).

Rebatching Soap

When I was a child, my very first money-saving project was rebatching soap. For some reason, I became obsessed with the fact that we buy soap, but then we throw a sliver away at the end of each bar. And while I had absolutely no problem returning a plate of half-eaten food to be thrown away after dinner, the idea of throwing away soap bothered me.

It still does. And while I don't make my own soap, I confess to having an old quart Mason jar in our supply cabinet in the bathroom where soap chips go to live when they are too small to use. Once the jar is full, the rebatching can begin!

First, you will want to save soap chips that are fairly small, about the size of the sliver that starts to get annoying to use. If you save big chunks, you will have trouble with this first step, although it isn't out of the question for you to grate those big chunks and hotel bars with a hand grater. But your first step is dumping all the soap (bit by bit) in your food processor and processing it until it is powdery. You will have some small chips left, but that is OK. Be sure to keep the lid on your food processor until the dust settles, because soap dust in the nose makes you sneeze like crazy! (I promise your food processor will clean up just fine with a trip or two through the dishwasher -- it is just soap, after all.)

If you don't fancy the idea of making new soap bars, you can stop here and use this powder as the first step in making homemade laundry soap. But I want new bars of soap, so I proceed.

Next, put your soap powder in a microwaveable bowl and cover just barely with water; you are going to melt the soap, but you don't want it to take forever to dry. Microwave it in minute-long bursts until you can see the majority of the powder has melted, which took me about 3-5 minutes total.

Finally, spread in a container of your choice. I plopped mine in an old cocoa container. Spread it out, and let it dry in a cool room until solid -- I stuck mine in the sunroom. Then, remove it from the container (this is where having a container with flexible sides and no lip helps), and allow it to further cure and dry until hard. Slice into bars, and you have recaptured the lost soap that you wasted over the course of time. For me, I got five "travel sized" bars out of the soap I've been saving for just over a year.

The Analysis

Fast: OK, not particularly. But not too bad; the project probably took me an hour total, plus drying time.

Cheap: If I had been forgoing paying work for my writing clients or my Carrot Creations yoga sock clients to do this, it might not have been a good deal. But I used free time, and I probably recouped a couple of bucks in soap costs.

Good: This is definitely a "because I can" kind of project, but I do enjoy the idea of saving my "lost" soap.

Passive Solar Heating

After enduring a Midwestern winter, these first warm days in the 50s are a blessing. They are also a golden opportunity to heat your house with an energy source you don't have to pay for: solar.

Even without expensive collectors and arrays, you can heat your house with passive solar energy, just by opening curtains and blinds on east-facing windows in the morning, and south- and west-facing windows in the afternoon. (I find the north-facing windows never collect that much sun, but that may have something to do with the construction/positioning of our house.)

Even with temps in the upper 40s at the start of the week, I am able to heat my house up to 64 degrees with passive solar, which is a degree above the 63 degree set point of my thermostat for daytime when I am feeling hard core about saving. In spring, I can turn the heat off during the day and just using it to "catch" the house at night so nothing freezes (including me).

The Analysis

Fast: Can't get much faster than opening those curtains!

Cheap: Every degree you heat your house by passive solar is one you don't pay for from the gas or electric company.

Good: Nothing prettier or nicer than a warm, bright house on a spring day, particularly when you don't have to pay for it!

In Praise of Shaving Soap

Gentlemen have a lot of choices when it comes to shaving. While most guys who came of age in the past fifty years probably reach for the can of shaving foam and the disposable safety razor, there is an option that is better for the planet and, more important, infinitely sexier: shaving soap.

Mr. FC&G uses old school shaving soap lathered on with a brush, which has the following advantages:

- Pricewise, there is not a bunch of difference between shaving soap and shaving foam. In our local grocery, any brand of shaving soap (and there are Williams, Colgate, and others) comes in a few cents less per cake than a can of the cheapest shaving foam. However, you do have the start-up costs of a shaving mug (I got Mr. FC&G a pretty one, but you can certainly demote one from your kitchen cabinet for free) and shaving brush (which seem to last almost forever, but you'll have to replace them occasionally in your lifetime). The cake soap seems to last much longer than a can of foam.

- As far as solid waste, the soap wins. A new cake of shaving soap comes in a small cardboard box. Shaving foam comes in a large metal can with plastic parts. No contest.

- Mr. FC&G says the soap gives a better shave than the foam.

- And this one is key: watching a man shave by foaming up with a brush and mug is undeniably hot. Think about it, guys.

The Analysis

Fast: I don't believe it takes any longer for Mr. FC&G to lather up with a brush than to spray foam in his hand. If so, we are talking a very small amount of time.

Cheap: Lifetime shaving expenditures are probably the same whether you use soap or foam. Any financial impact you realize will have to come from using razors with disposable blades and reusable handles and caring for them well to make them last.

Good: This tip is all about impact. A switch to shaving soap will mean less solid waste, a better shave, and perhaps an intrigued wife. Your call, guys!

A Few Words About Water

Water is a simple thing, but we still manage to spend a lot of time and money on it. Between transporting water and various beverages to the store, to spending good money on them, to transporting them to our home and storing them, we often devote a lot of resources to something that comes virtually free from our taps. Some ideas for cutting that expense:

1. Of course, we've said it before and the frugal blogosphere will say it again, but please do everything you can to avoid buying bottled water. It costs a lot to transport, both in money and environmental impact, leading to a big expenditure for you. It also throws off a lot of trash, which you have to haul to the curb and someone else has to haul to the landfill or recycling center. In this case, I'm going to advocate you spend to save: Go out right now and treat yourself to a stainless steel or aluminum water bottle that you will fill from your tap and carry with you to work or wherever you need water. If you don't trust your tap water (and most of us really have nothing to worry about), get whatever filtration system will make you feel secure about drinking your own tap water. Long term, these purchases will save you money.

2. While you're at it, stop buying bottled iced tea. You can make iced tea in about 10 seconds of work and an hour or so of waiting, just by filling a jar with warm water and throwing in one industrial-sized tea bag. Again, don't pay someone to transport water to you. (For those of you extra-worried about bacteria growth in "sun tea," just let it steep in the fridge.) The same logic goes for soda pop; get a home carbonation system, which are all the rage, and make your own pop. All you will have to pay for is the soda mix, which comes fairly cheap and in a very small bottle.

3. Finally, an odd water-related tip I read in a WWII-era home economics publication: when you use a carton of cream (or half-and-half, or a can of evaporated milk), rinse the container out with an ounce or two of water, and add this reconstituted milk to your milk jug or use it in cooking as milk. I thought this was a neat idea, and I've been doing this on the rare occasions that I have a container of

half-and-half around. It saves a couple of cents and gives me the jollies, which isn't a bad thing either.

Wood Ash: Recycling to the Nth Degree

Sometimes, I get an insane amount of pleasure out of a perfect system. The ideal example of this is my love for wood ash and the process that makes sure that nothing goes to waste.

It all starts with our fireplace insert and a stack of hardwood. Because we don't heat exclusively (or even primarily) with wood, we don't need several cord of it. Instead, we do just fine collecting and splitting our own tree trimmings and deadfall and buying wood from friends and neighbors who have removed a tree or had one fall in a storm. The project of splitting and sawing wood is a continual one, and it provides a great workout while enjoying the outdoors.

During the winter months, this wood helps heat the house some days, while also creating a nice warm nook for letting bread rise or making yogurt. We even bake potatoes in the Dutch oven, so the fire does double duty most of the time.

What we are left with is ash. And while this is already a relatively minimal amount of waste from a very efficient process, we take it one step further. I collect the ash into an old canner, then use it a scoop at a time in the bottom of my compost bucket. It serves to dehydrate and deodorize the food scraps, making the bucket more pleasant to deal with. It also makes it possible to skip a day or two between trips out to the compost pile on those snowy and icy days.

Ultimately, of course, the ash finally makes its way to the compost pile, where it contributes to creating the fertilizer that will help the garden thrive, giving us vegetables to nourish our bodies and give us the energy needed to saw and split more wood. The circle continues.

The Analysis

Fast: The most time-intensive part of this process is sawing and splitting logs, which takes a while, especially given that we still do it manually. However, if you recharacterize this in your own mind from "chore" to "workout" and put in half an hour three times a week all summer (and we don't do that much by any means), you will be in shape and have a monster pile of wood.

Cheap: We spend very little on wood, as neighbors with a downed tree are usually pretty generous about giving wood away if we will haul it. However, we do try to pay them when they will accept money.

Good: There is no waste in this process and benefit every step of the way. I enjoy this perhaps more than is healthy!

Selling Scrap Aluminum: Worth the Time?

When I was little, I had this thing about selling aluminum cans. My Dad and I would walk our neighborhood armed with a bag and a magnet to collect discarded cans. (Note to my younger readers: 1) This was during an era when "out the car window" was a perfectly acceptable method for disposing of trash, and 2) It was also when some beverage cans were part or all steel, so the magnet told us which were aluminum because it wouldn't attach to an aluminum can.) At least we didn't go so far as to pick up the pop tops. (Another note to my younger readers: Cans used to come with pop tops that removed and were discarded separately. You can Google that if you want to find out exactly what Jimmy Buffett stepped on when he blew out his flip-flop.)

Anyway, once I had a bag full of cans, Mom would drive me to the aluminum collection point. As I remember, this was only available periodically at rotating collection points, like the firehouse one month and somewhere else another. My days as scrap metal entrepreneur ended one day when the rotating collection point was difficult to find, and, after a morning of driving around town, I became car sick. Let's just say that Mom did a little environmental impact calculation of her own and vetoed the project.

Anyway, Mr. FC&G and I have recently started collecting our own scrap aluminum, which is mostly pop cans. And while the most economical thing to do is to just avoid soda entirely, we thought this was a good way to recoup some of our costs on this junk food luxury.

And the answer is: I'm divided. After several months, we had $21 of aluminum, most of it from cans, but part from some industrial scrap aluminum that Mr. FC&G also sold. As it turns out, the cans net the most per pound (78 cents, at this writing) because they are a known composition and grade, but they don't weigh up very fast. It is only a marginally practical endeavor because the scrap dealer is located on the way to work for Mr. FC&G (so no extra transportation costs), and because he is still selling off industrial scrap. I think once the industrial stuff is gone, saving cans may not be a great use of our time.

The Analysis

Fast: Throwing cans in a bin is easy, but you do have to factor in time to crush them and sell them. I estimate that therefore we probably made $5-7 an hour on this one.

Cheap: Cheap, or cheapskate? While I still love the idea of making money from something I would otherwise "donate" to my curbside trash/recycling service, this has to be a low priority project. Anything else is not an efficient use of time.

Good: Then again, I do really like the $21 in my farmer's market jar, which is a jar of cash that we keep for farmer's market trips. There is nothing worse than seeing an array of seasonal berries and local, cage-free chicken meat and realizing you have $10 in your wallet. At least I will turn something unhealthy (pop) into something very healthy.

Sustainable Tool: The Santoku Knife

As an avid gardener, food preserver, and almost-vegetarian, I chop a lot of veggies. And, I have amassed a lot of paring knives, ranging from expensive to dead cheap. (In fact, my favorite paring knife is one that DH picked up at a big box retailer when he was out of town on business; I think he said it cost $3.) On top of that, like most brides, I registered for the obligatory butcher block knife set when we married. So, like most people of my age, I now have a drawer full of knives, each supposedly doing a different job, and each taking up space and having cost money.

All I needed to start was a santoku knife.

The santoku knife is a Japanese-inspired (the real ones are Japanese), relatively flat-bladed knife with these little divots along the side. The divots are what is magic; they keep the knife from sticking to the food, and therefore you can slice much more easily through whatever you are cutting. Although I gather it is primarily a vegetable knife, it is definitely my first choice for cutting cheese or meat these days. In fact, I usually don't put this one in the dishwasher but instead just wash it off and put it back in the drawer. (I know, I know: you shouldn't put knives in the dishwasher at all. But I am usually too lazy not to, so I have to work with my own reality here.)

I wish I had known about the santoku knife earlier, before I started amassing a collection of knives for all occasion. If you are reading this and just starting to amass kitchen tools, I recommend you acquire knives in the following order:

1. A santoku knife. Pick a medium sized one that fits comfortably in your hand.
2. A paring knife. There are still a few things too small to do with the medium santoku.
3. A bread knife. The serrated edge will cut bread, cake, and other such things.
4. A set of (usually six) steak knives. This gives you good meat knives for four people with two left over to use to cut meat in the kitchen.

That's it! If you are just setting up housekeeping, you can certainly get by a long time on just the first two, then add the last two. You only need specialty knives, like a meat cleaver, if you are doing a specialty job frequently. For example, I would keep my strawberry knife with the little curved tip, because it does such a good job of hulling strawberries and cutting stem ends out of tomatoes with minimal waste.

The Analysis

Fast: Your "fast" benefit here is that you will have a far easier time cutting things with a santoku, so you save time there. You also will have an easier time finding it in a drawer if you limit your knives.

Cheap: I got my santoku knife for about $7 at Meijer. You can spend a ton, but you really don't need to. (Don't tell the foodies I said that!) If you are starting out, you can probably get the first three knives for under $25 total; this is a good thing to put on your wish list too, if you have people wanting seasonal hints.

Good: Limiting clutter with a good-feeling tool is always a pleasure.

Adding on to Your Abode: Our "Key West" Sunroom

In 2010, the circumstances were finally right for us to enclose our covered patio to make a sunroom. This sunroom/greenhouse is affectionately known around here as the "Key West Room" because of our use of the island as inspiration for the decor. I think it is a great case study for how to make decisions about additions to your home.

First, let me acknowledge that adding onto a house is not necessarily economical; every estimate I have seen indicates that home owners will only rarely recover 100% of the cost of an addition or renovation in the resale of their house, and I'm sure that is true in a recessionary housing market. However, we opted to add this sunroom because it would extend the true living area of our home, which is the kitchen, family room, patio (now sunroom) and gardens. We opted for a sunroom instead of, perhaps, a pool or a media room, because it would be a highly functional space. We also opted to wait until we had met certain financial goals we had, and until we had the money in hand, so that is why we owned this house for ten years without adding a sunroom that we knew we wanted.

The footprint of the new room already existed on the house. The back patio was already covered by existing roofline, and the concrete pad of the patio nestled under the roof in an "L" of the house. Therefore, we were literally two walls short of a room. The concrete pad even already had a footer in place, so, by keeping to this existing footprint instead of extending out into the gardens (heaven forbid!), we had the most economical option possible.

We chose a patio room company that had two options: a three-season room wall system and a four-season system. The four season option was sturdier and better insulated, so we opted to go that direction. The room could easily be heated with a space heater, or baseboard heat could be installed if we wish. However, we don't intend for the room to be additional winter living space, so we have not gone that route.

We chose walls that were part slider and part transom window. The transoms allow us to better control air flow, and they should allow us to use the room effectively on rainy days. We enjoy using the room on a cool day with just one or two transoms open for ventilation, and the room stays surprisingly warm even in the depths of winter.

The walls are a unique configuration designed by my husband. Each wall has a sliding panel and a fixed panel. Mr. FC&G requested that the fixed panels include the UV protection and the sliding panels allow full spectrum light. That way, in the cool months, we can position our indoor crops and seedlings in front of the full spectrum windows and use the space as a greenhouse; these windows will also allow for more passive solar heat to come in to warm the space. During the summer, when the sliders are back behind the fixed panels, the UV protection of those panels will keep the room a bit cooler. A ceiling fan we already installed will also help with ventilation.

So far, the room is functioning just as we intended. In lieu of a "Fast, Cheap, and Good" analysis, let me offer the following benefits from the addition of the room:

- Because of the unique combination of window glass detailed above, we have extended the growing season considerably. I can reliably grow greens and potatoes all winter long, while keeping some hearty herbs and our miniature apple trees healthy and getting good sunlight. I can also start more seedlings in the spring for the summer garden, since the space I have to work in is much larger than just kitchen counters and interior south-facing windows. The addition of a hanging grow light really helps during darker winter days.

- The room is acting now as a heat collector and a really good buffer between the family room doors and the outdoor temps. I have noticed the family room, to which this room connects, being warmer and cozier. On some warm days, we have opened the interior door and allowed the sunroom to heat the family room. Likewise, we can open the interior door on a cool summer night and flood the lower level of the house with fresh, cool air.

- We added a removable clothes line to run diagonally across the space, so I am able to hang sheets and other large items to air dry. They dry more quickly than in my lower level laundry room on drying racks. This will save a little money by allowing me to avoid running the drier.

- By choosing the four season wall option, we qualified for a tax credit. This lowered the price of the room dramatically. (The credit should be just shy of 20% of the room's cost.)

- I also paid for the room on a credit card that earned reward certificates; with these, I was able to get a set of flannel sheets for our bed (retail price $65.90) for only $5.90. So, that will keep us warm this year as well.

- Finally, we joke around here about the savings realized by not having to buy antidepressants in the winter. Truly, for us, having a sheltered space to take in more winter sunlight and garden plants makes a huge difference in mood and quality of life.

Jennifer Patterson Lorenzetti

8 Preparing for the Worst

A close cousin of the sustainability movement is the "prepper" movement, a mindset that holds that households should be prepared for emergencies ranging from a two-hour power outage to a hurricane to an economic depression, even up to an electromagnetic pulse that wipes out computer-driven machinery permanently and plunges the country back several decades if not a couple of centuries.

Preparing for the worst of these is beyond the scope of my book, but being prepared for the emergencies that might befall you is a good use of your time and energy. This chapter includes a few ideas that might get you thinking about your own preps.

On Being Prepared: Diary of the 2011 Ice Storm

Day One

Today was the first day of an anticipated two-day storm that has been called both "record-breaking" and "catastrophic." Mr. FC&G and I woke up at 6:15, and he immediately looked out the window and then went down to check on the condition of the driveway and streets. I grabbed the iPhone and powered up Twitter long enough to find that the college was closed and by the time I was finished, Mr. FC&G was back. "It's slicker than snot on a doorknob," he said and dived back under the quilts with me for another hour. When I got up, I knew this was the perfect day to share with you some of my thoughts on preparedness.

If you search online for sites dedicated to preparedness, you are in for a full afternoon or six reading various people's thoughts about how to prepare for situations ranging from bad to worse. Many people couch their preparation efforts in terms of events that they wish to be prepared to handle, whether that is job loss, dramatic inflation, political unrest, extreme weather, or even less-likely events. While the chances of any one thing going wrong may be small to infinitesimal, the chances over a lifetime that you are going to have to deal with a period of going off the grid, being separated from modern conveniences, or having an emergency that you have to handle yourself are pretty great. Being able to do so is part of living a self-sufficient, sustainable life.

Think you'll never need to be prepared to rough it a little? In just the last five years, I've had to deal with the breakage and replacement of a sewer pipe, a fender-bender that left me without transportation, the tail end of Hurricane Ike, and now the great ice storm of 2011. Each of these situations has benefited from me being prepared in various ways, and all were more or less unforeseeable in the long term. So, I'm not the type to prepare for a specific situation. Rather, I suggest you begin your preparedness efforts by looking at the amount of time you could possibly be "off the grid," separated from one or more of your conveniences. Let's look at some examples:

Less than an Hour: The power goes out to your home in a random thunderstorm. Do you know where your flashlight is? Your spare set of car keys? Can you find first aid supplies and any medications you may need in the dark? If you are at work, do you have enough gas in your car to get home? Is it safer to stay at work? How would you decide? Is your cell phone charged?

More than an Hour but Less than a Day: You lose power in an ice storm like we're having today. Do you have back-up heat that doesn't rely on electricity? Where are your extra quilts? Do you have enough food in the house to make a meal without a stove? What do you have to drink? Will your freezer stay cold for 24 hours so that you don't lose what you have stored? Do you have a hand-crank emergency radio so you can get updates? How about some candles?

A Day to a Week: Hurricane Ike took us off the grid for over four days. How will you prepare meals? Do you have a week's worth of food stored; if not, what if groceries are unavailable in the store? Do you consistently keep enough gas in your car for an emergency supply run if the gas stations are unavailable? How will you reach friends and family who are worried? Where's your passport? You might not be travelling internationally, but it is the best form of ID we currently have. Do you think you need a generator, a heater, a water purification system?

A Period of Months: A job loss, a hyperinflation, or (heaven forbid) a system collapse of some sort occurs. What survival skills do you have? Can you grow or trade for food? Do you know how to repair things around your house? What medical skills and supplies do you need? How much can you rely on your neighbors; how much do you want them to rely on you?

None of this is intended to frighten you. The more extreme the imagined circumstance, the less likely it is to occur. However, it is a good exercise to imagine scenarios that could leave you without your normal resources. Start with short term losses of one resource like, as mentioned above, a power outage for a limited period. Work your way up to more long-term and widespread problems. Discuss plans with your family. It might be a good idea to write down your plan, then revisit it occasionally.

Postscript: How did we prepare for this storm? We are in pretty good shape, considering we have a lot of stored food from the summer, piles of quilts, a snowblower, a pile of wood and a fireplace insert/stove. We charged the phones and got an extra can of gas and some kerosene for the heater. Mr. FC&G ran to the store for some comfort food items, but we would be OK for many days without. And so far, we are snug and warm in a house that still has power. We may not need any of our preparation items, but we'll use up our stock and then restock as needed. Being prepared and not needing it is far better than doing without.

Day Two

So, the second wave of the Great Ice Storm of 2011 has blown through, and we indeed lost power for 12 hours. So, I thought I'd report on the effectiveness of some of our preparedness.

The power went out just before 10 pm last night, and I immediately asked Mr. FC&G if he wanted me to make an olive oil lamp. I bought the parts for my olive oil lamps from Lehman's right after Hurricane Ike, and to be honest, I felt pretty darn stupid doing so. I have candles and flashlights, so what was I thinking gearing up to build emergency lamps? But last night, I was thrilled to have done so. Right now you can buy a pack of 6 wicks and inserts for $18.95; you provide your own mason jar. Mason jars are the best container because they can handle heat well. Basically, the inserts and wicks come in a very small bag that I tucked in a drawer until the time came to use them. Once I had put together a couple of lamps, I found that they created a much brighter light than candles with virtually no smoke or odor. (When you blow them out, there is a faint odor that reminded me of fried chicken.)

Mr. FC&G also showed his true preparedness cred by reminding me that he had a stock of Boy Scout camping gear in the garage if we needed to cook, and he remembered to let the faucets drip to keep the pipes from freezing. He also really took one for the team in the form of getting up every two hours to check the pipes and looking to see if any trees had fallen. I snuck downstairs at 7 am and threw another quilt over him on the couch.

Finally, I have to comment on how helpful Facebook was in this emergency. While it is probably not a long-term communication solution in a big emergency, I really appreciated seeing everyone across town and across the country reporting on power outages and causes. I knew a transmitter had blown in the neighboring town almost immediately as it happened and significantly before the media reported it.

Sustainable Tool: Mortar and Pestle

A few years ago, Hurricane Ike barreled up from the Gulf and continued north until it hit Ohio as a Category 1 Hurricane. Most of you probably laugh at the idea of a category one storm being memorable, but let me assure you that a mostly-landlocked Midwestern state has done very little hurricane preparedness work. We were left without power for nearly a week, and that event kicked off my interest in finding tools that can be used off the grid.

One of my favorite such tools, although it wouldn't have done much in a temporary power outage like Ike caused, is the mortar and pestle. You may recognize the iconic shape from apothecary signs at your local pharmacy, and that is no accident. A mortar and pestle is the original grinding tool. It can be used to grind and compound (mix) medications, hence the link with pharmacies, but it has traditionally been used to grind herbs and spices and crack grains and nuts. I use mine several times a week during food preservation season for just these tasks.

I can't tell you the pleasure that this tool brings me. It allows me to quickly and easily grind, powder, and crush herbs, seeds, and herbal medications in a way that has been done for millennia. Think of that - you are doing a task that someone could have done before electricity, before the railroad, even before writing. This tool is so basic, just picking one up links you with history. (That kind of gives me a little chill, but I am a history nerd that way.)

It also does the job well. I recommend you buy one made of stone; mine is marble, but there are granite ones available. Get one with a smooth interior, although it doesn't have to be polished. Place a little of what you are grinding inside, then take the pestle (which I just learned derives from the Latin for "pounder") and start by pressing against your substance, then working up to something slightly more intense than tapping. You don't want to imitate the Flintstones and pick the pestle up and slam it against the mortar.

Also, with a mortar and pestle, you can forget about the conventional foodie recommendation to buy a separate coffee grinder and use it just for grinding spices, so the spice flavor doesn't contaminate the coffee. With a stone mortar and pestle, you can grind any flavorful substance and then wipe it clean with no flavor residue. You may want to use a drop or two of dish washing liquid if you just worked with hot peppers, but otherwise you can clean your mortar and pestle with water and a clean towel.

I have a possibly unreasonable love for this tool. With proper care, it will be with me for a lifetime. Maybe in a millennium, someone else will think of me while they preserve their food using a mortar and pestle.

Jennifer Patterson Lorenzetti

Appendix: Index

Apple Sauce, 117
Baking Supplies, 143
Basil Pesto, 64
Bed Warmers, 130
Boring Stuff, 8
Broadfork, 34
Butternut Squash Soup, 70
Canning, 102
Cheesy Potato Soup, 66
Cherries, Freezing, 105
Chicken, Roast, 99
Chili Sauce, WWII, 111
Cilantro, Freezing, 104
Compost, 30
Coupons, 141
Croutons, 48
Cucumber Trellis, 33
Dried Tomatoes, 107
Ersatz Cotton Balls, 120
Fall Linen Washing, 138
Fleece Patchwork "(Un)quilt",
   133
Fleece Pillowcases, 122
Food Preservation, 101
Forage, 24
French Bread, 45
Front Yard, 11
Gardening, 27
Gnocchi, Pumpkin, 53
Hand Warmers, 132
Hankies, 128
Health, 6
Heat, 18
History, 4
Holidays, 20
Hot Toddy, Mr. FC&G's, 42

Household Helps, 135
Ice Storm, 164
Introduction, 1
Ketchup, 113
Knowing How, 12
Laundry Soap, 144
Lavender, 109
Mojito Salmon, 93
Mojito, Jen's Perfect, 40
Money, 6
Mortar and Pestle, 168
Natural Resources, 7
Orecchiette Au Gratin, 56
Oregano, Dried, 110
Organization, 14
Part-Time Job, 22
Passive Solar Heating, 148
Pasta, Homemade, 51
Pepper Seeds, 28
Pesto-dressed Pasta, 61
Philosophy, 5
Pie Crust, Mr. FC&G's Flaky,
   80
Poor Man's Latte, 38
Pork Sausage, 96
Potato Salad, Blue, 63
Potatoes, Red, White, and
   Blue, 74
Preparing, 163
Ravioli, Pumpkin, 58
Rebatching Soap, 146
Reusable Swiffer Cloths, 124
Sage Noodle Soup, 68
Salmon Patties, 95
Santoku Knife, 157
Sauteed Root Veggies, 77

Scrap Aluminum, 155
Shaving Soap, 149
Simple Syrup, 43
Smoothies, 86
Snow-Washing, 136
Sour Cream, Homemade, 89
Spoonbread, 50
Squash, 36
Steam-Cleaning, 139
Stock, 91
Stretching, 16
Sunroom, 159
Sustainability, 6

Textiles, 119
Thai Basil Salmon, 84
Time, 6
Tomato Sauce, 115
Tortellini and Four Cheese
    Sauce, 55
Wash Cloths, 126
Waste, 10
Water, 151
Whipped Butternut Squash, 72
Wood Ash, 153
Yogurt, 87
Zucchini Pie, 78

ABOUT THE AUTHOR

Jennifer Patterson Lorenzetti had her first garden – and her first compost pile – at the age of eight. Armed with vintage canning recipes from her grandmother and great-aunt, she began her journey toward sustainable homemaking, adding skills in textile arts, food preparation, and savvy shopping and budgeting. In 1997, she founded Hilltop Communications, a writing and speaking firm dedicated to making complex topics accessible for a variety of audiences and through a variety publications and venues. She has written hundreds of articles for a variety of clients, and her work has received a TABBIE Honorable Mention for Best Technical Article. In 2009, she married the two passions and started "Fast, Cheap, and Good," the blog that draws on her experiences as a writer and homemaker dedicated to pursuing a better life with fewer resources. She is available for writing, speaking, and consulting.

Follow this blog at
fastcheapandgood.blogspot.com

Learn more about the author at
www.hilltopcommunications.net

www.ingramcontent.com/pod-product-compliance
Lightning Source LLC
Chambersburg PA
CBHW061144040426
42445CB00013B/1545